HISTORY AS
SOCIAL SCIENCE

THE BEHAVIORAL AND SOCIAL SCIENCES SURVEY
History Panel

David S. Landes, *Chairman*
Harvard University

Charles Tilly, *Co-Chairman*
University of Michigan

Howard F. Cline
Library of Congress

Sigmund Diamond
Columbia University

Samuel P. Hays
University of Pittsburgh

Thomas C. Smith
University of California, Berkeley

HISTORY AS SOCIAL SCIENCE

Edited by
David S. Landes and Charles Tilly

A SPECTRUM BOOK

Prentice-Hall, Inc., *Englewood Cliffs*, N. J.

Current printing (last number):
10 9 8 7 6 5 4 3 2 1

Prentice-Hall International, Inc. (*London*)
Prentice-Hall of Australia, Pty. Ltd. (*Sydney*)
Prentice-Hall of Canada, Ltd. (*Toronto*)
Prentice-Hall of India Private Limited (*New Delhi*)
Prentice-Hall of Japan, Inc. (*Tokyo*)

FOREWORD

This book is one of a series prepared in connection with the Survey of the Behavioral and Social Sciences conducted between 1967 and 1969 under the auspices of the Committee on Science and Public Policy of the National Academy of Sciences and the Problems and Policy Committee of the Social Science Research Council.

The Survey provides a comprehensive review and appraisal of these rapidly expanding fields of knowledge, and constitutes a basis for an informed, effective national policy to strengthen and develop these fields even further.

The reports in the Survey, each the work of a panel of scholars, include studies of anthropology, economics, geography, history as a social science, political science, psychology, psychiatry as a behavioral science, sociology, and the social science aspects of statistics, mathematics and computation. A general volume discusses relations among the disciplines, broad questions of utilization of the social sciences by society, and makes specific recommendations for public and university policy.

While close communication among all concerned has been the rule, the individual panel reports are the responsibility of the panels producing them. They have not been formally reviewed or approved by the Central Planning Committee or by the sponsoring organizations: They were reviewed at an earlier stage by representatives of the National Academy of Sciences and the Social Science Research Council.

Much of the data on the behavioral and social sciences in universities used in these reports comes from a 1968 questionnaire survey, conducted by the Survey Committee, of universities offering the PhD in one of these fields. Questionnaires were filled out by PhD-granting departments (referred to as the Departmental Questionnaire); by selected professional schools (referred to as the Professional School Questionnaire); by computation centers (referred to as the Computation Center Questionnaire); by university financial offices (referred to as the Administration Questionnaire); and by research institutes, centers, laboratories and museums engaged in research in the behavioral and social sciences (referred to as the Institute Questionnaire). Further information concerning this questionnaire survey is provided in the appendix to the general report of the Central Planning Committee, *The Behavioral and Social Sciences: Outlook and Needs.*

Also included in the appendix of the report of the Central Planning Committee is a discussion of the method of degree projection used in these reports, as well as some alternative methods.

THE BEHAVIORAL AND SOCIAL SCIENCES SURVEY COMMITTEE
CENTRAL PLANNING COMMITTEE

Ernest R. Hilgard, *Stanford University*, CHAIRMAN
Henry W. Riecken, *Social Science Research Council*, CO-CHAIRMAN
Kenneth E. Clark, *University of Rochester*
James A. Davis, *Dartmouth College*
Fred R. Eggan, *The University of Chicago*
Heinz Eulau, *Stanford University*
Charles A. Ferguson, *Stanford University*
John L. Fischer, *Tulane University of Louisiana*
David A. Hamburg, *Stanford University*
Carl Kaysen, *Institute for Advanced Study*
William H. Kruskal, *The University of Chicago*
David S. Landes, *Harvard University*
James G. March, *University of California, Irvine*
George A. Miller, *The Rockefeller University*
Carl Pfaffmann, *The Rockefeller University*
Neil J. Smelser, *University of California, Berkeley*
Allan H. Smith, *Washington State University*
Robert M. Solow, *Massachusetts Institute of Technology*
Edward Taaffe, *The Ohio State University*
Charles Tilly, *The University of Michigan*
Stephen Viederman, *National Academy of Sciences*, EXECUTIVE OFFICER

CONTENTS

PREFACE

The following report is part of a larger survey of the behavioral and social sciences and undertaken at the request of the National Academy of Sciences and the Social Science Research Council. In accordance with the terms of this inquiry and in response to its objectives, the report on history has concerned itself primarily with those persons, within and without the historical profession, who are in whole or in part engaged in work of a social science character and with that part of historical study and training that falls within the scope of social science. This focus has no invidious implications. On the contrary, it is the conviction of the editors of the report that the diversity of historical work is a reflection of the diversity of the historian's interests and the evidence available to him and that this diversity is a valuable, even indispensable feature of the discipline. The different kinds of historians need and stimulate one another.

Because history is not a unitary discipline, however, an inquiry of this kind assumes a special character. It can not be simply addressed by the profession to the outside world. Instead it is addressed on behalf of one segment of the profession to both the discipline and the outside world. We are trying to convey the state of that part of history that is or would be social science, and to offer recommendations that would promote and improve this kind of work for those who want to do it.

This improvement is in the interest of all historians. The changing character of historical evidence, the development of new techniques and concepts in related disciplines, the growing body of research by nonhistorians into historical problems—all of these imply that even those historians who are not themselves working in social science have to learn to read it and use it, if only to teach their students. What is more, most of the material facilities required to promote social-scientific history are by their nature facilities for the entire discipline. Better libraries, easier retrieval and dissemination of data, more generous arrangements for pre- and postdoctoral research, and similar improvements redound directly or indirectly to the benefit of all.

In return, these gains are dependent on the cooperation of all, for students of history as social science will always need training in all aspects of the discipline. If anything, the growing sophistication of social-scientific techniques makes it all the more important for practitioners of these techniques to know and appreciate the humanistic approach to historical knowledge. We cannot afford to gain a world of numbers and models and lose our historical souls in the process.

Although the theme of this report is focused on, and is the expression of, one segment of the historical profession, the report is the distillation of diverse points of view. The authors of the report are all working historians of one variety or another. Some of us are closely identified with outside disciplines, such as economics or sociology. Others of us employ little or none of the apparatus of social science in our day-to-day work. Our experiences and our commitments differ. In the course of writing, moreover, we have consulted widely with colleagues of all styles and persuasions. (A list of those who have been kind enough to help us is given in the acknowledgments.) This consultation modified our convictions in some areas and reinforced them in others; it did not erase them. It made us aware, in particular, of the immense diversity of historical theory and practice in the United States. Needless to say, these numerous consultants bear no responsibility for the report that follows or the use made of their opinions.

There is already a large body of literature on the method and nature of history, and there have been in recent years a number of essays on the relation of history to social science. Many of these raise difficult epistemological questions about the nature of truth and evidence that we prefer to avoid. We have barely touched the classic questions of historical knowledge: To what degree can the historian ever free himself from the biases of his own time and place? Should he? Is there a special mode of historical knowledge based on empathy —the ability to put oneself into the skins of other people in other times and places? Are there laws, cycles, repetitions, or irreversible trends in history? Nor have we seriously examined the role of historical thinking and materials outside the discipline of history—an important question in a day when economists, sociologists, political scientists, and many others are attempting to work with historical evidence. Instead, we have concentrated our attention on history as a discipline and a profession, with special attention to the social-scientific sector, loosely defined. The kinds of questions we ask are: Who are the historians? What do they do? How do they work? What do they want and need? And what can be done about it?

The first large section of the report treats the discipline of history in general and seeks to define the characteristics of social-scientific history in terms of ideal types. It includes summary findings of a survey of about 600 working historians, which the panel undertook in the spring of 1968; the survey is described in greater detail in the appendix. The next section describes some of the varieties of social-scientific history, their achievements, limitations, and promise. Then we turn to the resources, working, and needs of the profession—first in teaching, then in research. A special section is devoted to the library problem, another to the role of foreign scholars. Finally, we sum up the observations and recommendations made along the way.

ACKNOWLEDGMENTS

John Higham (University of Michigan) left the History Panel in July, 1967, but did not cease to maintain good relations with the members or to offer good advice when asked. Paul Alexander (University of California, Berkeley), who could not agree with some of the recommendations in the report, resigned at the end of 1969 after doing an important part of the preparatory work. All the other members participated in drafting sections of the report, but Landes and Tilly took responsibility for preparing the final version. A review committee consisting of Felix Gilbert (Institute for Advanced Study), Cyril Stanley Smith (Massachusetts Institute of Technology), James W. Prothro (University of North Carolina), and David Potter (Stanford University) offered vigorous and useful criticism of an intermediate draft. From within the Behavioral and Social Sciences Survey Committee, Henry David, Henry Riechen, and Stephen Viederman provided useful information and benevolent advice. The panel received preparatory memos from Samuel H. Beer (Harvard), Robert Bellah (University of California, Berkeley), Lee Benson (University of Pennsylvania), Robert Butow (University of Washington), Robert Cross (Swarthmore College), Philip D. Curtin (University of Wisconsin), Peter Duignan (The Hoover Institution), John K. Fairbank (Harvard University), Albert Feuerwerker (University of Michigan), Albert Fishlow (University of California, Berkeley), Robert Fogel (University of Chicago), Peter Gould (Pennsylvania State University), Erich Gruen (University of California, Berkeley), John G. Gurley (Stanford University), Herbert G. Gutman (University of Rochester), John Hall (Yale University), J. H. Hexter (Yale University), Richard Jensen (Washington University, St. Louis), Wesley Johnson (Stanford University), Sherman Kent (Washington, D.C.), Thomas Kuhn (Princeton University), Carl Leban (University of Kansas), Joseph Levenson (University of California, Berkeley), William W. Lockwood (Princeton University), Mark Mancall (Stanford University), Seymour Mandelbaum (University of Pennsylvania), Byron Marshall (University of Minnesota), Helen McCullough (Stanford University), William McCullough (Stanford University), Maurice Meisner (University of Virginia), Rowland Mitchell (Social Science Research Council), James William Morley (Columbia University), Frederic Mote (Princeton University), Murray Murphey (University of Pennsylvania), David Nivison (Stanford University), E. G. Pulleyblank (University of British Columbia), Carl Schorske (Princeton University), Boyd Shafer (Macalester College), Gilbert Shapiro (University of Pittsburgh), James Sheridan (Northwestern University), Bernard Silberman (University of Arizona), Thomas Skidmore (University of Wisconsin), Lawrence Stone (Princeton University), Ronald Syme (Cambridge University), Peter Temin (Massachusetts Institute of Technology), Stephan Thernstrom (University of California, Los Angeles), Frederic Wakeman (University of California, Berkeley), Paul Ward (American Historical Association), Arthur F. Wright (Yale University), Liensheng Yang (Harvard University); we thank them for their help. We are also grateful to the hundreds of historians who replied to the questionnaire distributed in 1968. Since we guaranteed them anonymity, their responses appear without citation throughout the report. None of our many counselors can be held responsible for the statements or misstatements to follow; only Landes and Tilly saw the last version of the text before it went to press.

1
WHAT IS HISTORY?

History is, first of all, the custodian of the collective memory and as such performs the important function of nourishing the collective ego. Second, it is in all societies a primary vehicle of the socialization of the young, teaching them the past so that they may know who they are and behave appropriately in the present. Third, it is the branch of inquiry that seeks to arrive at an accurate account and valid understanding of the past.

The third function is in large part a response to and corrective of the other two. Precisely because history has critical social, psychological, and educational functions; precisely because we are all prisoners of our past, in the sense that our options are limited by what has gone before and our preferences are shaped by our image of who we are and have been, it is of the utmost importance that we try to free our history from myth and error. Otherwise we are liable to self-deception or manipulation. It is no coincidence that authoritarian regimes have typically found it desirable and even necessary to censor works of history and to rewrite the record of the past to their convenience and advantage; that even democratic societies have chosen history texts for their children that would inculcate sentiments of pride and patriotism; or that the "emerging nations" of today, like those of yesterday, should all be engaged in a systematic effort to recreate (or create) their past in order to enhance their present and future.

The attempt to eschew the path of indoctrination or self-delusion, to develop history as an intellectual discipline seeking an objective truth independent of the seeker, is a typically Western rationalistic response to a problem that most other cultures have treated very differently. We are a historicist civilization. Our sacred books—the Old and New Testaments—are essentially histories, as are some of the oldest and greatest of our literary classics. By common consent, the greatest of the ancient historians was Thucydides, whose claim to immortality rests in large part on his efforts to free himself from romanticism and myth and to treat history not as a source of passion and psychic gratification but rather as a doorway to experience and wisdom.

Further, Western civilization is optimistic. We have almost un-limited faith in man's ability to know and, by knowing, to do. This almost narcissistic confidence in ourselves has had its greatest con-firmation in the realms of natural science and technology. By con-trast, our relative ignorance of human behavior and our impotence in dealing with it are lamentable; even so, we cherish the conviction that as we know more, we shall do better; and in that case, we shall never do better unless we know more.

Know more about what? Every one of the social sciences has its own contribution to make to our knowledge of man. The contribu-tion of history is *perspective*. This is no small matter. It is only too easy and too tempting for each generation, especially the more sensitive members of each generation, to see the tests and troubles of their own time as unique. For many, what is past is past, and what matters is now and sometimes later. This is particularly true of social engineers, who, however much they may be motivated by the recollection of past *wrongs*, do not want to be discouraged by the record of past *mistakes*. In defense of this "ostrich approach," it must be admitted that history has been misused as a stick to beat reformers and to block change. Yet never is the perspective of history so valuable as when men try to shape their destiny, that is, try to change history. Then, if ever, man has to know how he came to this pass; otherwise he is condemned to repeat his errors or, at best, to blunder through one difficulty only to arrive at another. In this sense, history, if read correctly, should help make men wise.

Not everyone would agree. There has always been a body of opinion within the historical profession that has denied the pos-sibility of an objective history—for the very cogent reason that it is simply impossible for the historian to perceive the past except through eyes distorted by personal values and sympathies. Each man, in this view, is his own historian. As for the lessons of history, men choose these to their purpose—like the devil citing scripture. De Gaulle called on France's tradition of greatness and power to justify his break with NATO; his adversaries pointed to the experience of two world wars to show the necessity of European cooperation. Israelis cite Jewish history to demonstrate the justice and passion of their attachment to the Holy Land; Palestinians point to their own history —as recorded in the Bible—to argue that they were there first. Supporters of the American military intervention in Vietnam have drawn an analogy to Munich and the appeasement of the 1930s to justify firmness in the face of totalitarian aggression; while their opponents have gone back to ancient Athens for lessons in the folly of arrogance. History is not alone in this respect: one could cite any number of other examples of self-serving analogy, even of conflicting inferences from the same body of evidence, from any of the behavioral and social sciences. A lawyer might even remark that this is the human condition: people will always see things differently; that's what keeps the courts busy.

It would be a serious mistake, however, to infer from these difficulties that our ignorance is inevitable and irreducible. Just as courts have developed over time adversary procedures and principles of evidence designed to promote the pursuit of truth and justice, so the social sciences, including history, have invented techniques for the collection, verification, and appraisal of evidence as a means of understanding man's motivations and behavior. The social scientist shares in the understanding that results cannot be complete or definitive: he typically deals in a realm of probability; but as his techniques have become more refined and powerful, the probabilities and usefulness of his answers have increased. The gains have been greatest in those areas where the social scientist has been able to simplify his problems by exclusion of all but a few paramount variables; the best example is economics. History, by comparison, has and will always have a hard time: the matter to be studied is inherently complex (some would say, infinitely complex) and resistant to simplification. That, however, only makes the task harder and the results of inquiry necessarily looser. It does not rule out a closer approach to the goal of truth.

History is no different from other intellectual disciplines in having to fulfill several roles at once; but it is more multifarious and hence more divided than the others. There is no such thing as an introductory core course that aims to convey the essence of the subject.

Nor is there any pretense to an orthodoxy—whether in the problems to study, the methods to employ, or the standards to meet. Because of this highly valued freedom from norms, the range of performance is extremely wide. Thus, although history is first and foremost a story—and to this day this is what the average person thinks of as history—there are all kinds of stories: dull or exciting, scrupulously careful or wildly imaginative, painfully naive or subtly interpretive. At one extreme is the simple chronicle that strings events one after the other like separate stones on the strand of time; at the other is the account that tries to explain each event as the result of what went before, including in the explanation such enduring circumstances, environmental and internal, as influence the behavior of the actors in the story. Needless to say, most histories fall not at the extremes, but somewhere between.

The same range of variation is found in that kind of history that treats, not of a sequence of change through time, but of a state of affairs or the condition of persons at a moment in time. At one extreme is the antiquarian approach, which simply collects bits and pieces of data, more or less without regard to their importance or interrelationships. At the other is the highly schematized or focused analytical model, which is all articulation and interrelationships. Again, most descriptive histories fall somewhere in between.

In general the bulk of historical work takes these forms, that is, narration of a sequence of events or description of persons and circumstances. A survey of articles published in the *American Historical Review* at intervals from 1901 to 1963 shows almost two-thirds to be of this type, and while this proportion would be lower in some of the more specialized journals (in fields like economic history, for example), it would be higher in local and regional periodicals. By comparison, only about 10 percent took the form of systematic analyses or explanations of historical phenomena, with the remainder devoted to questions of historical method and critiques of research. The contrast in this regard with social science disciplines like anthropology and sociology is worth noting. In anthropology, descriptive articles in the *American Anthropologist*, which accounted for almost four-fifths of the total in the first years of this century, have become steadily less important, until they now represent less than half the work published; while articles of the explanatory type have risen from a tenth to about a third. In sociology, descriptive pieces have maintained themselves at about a third of the total; but critical essays, which once accounted for 55 percent, have lost steadily in importance to about 15 percent, while analytical work has tripled in importance.[1]

Can one, within these families of historical subject matter, distinguish the historian as social scientist from other historians? Not easily. Many if not most historians are unwilling to be categorized in this way. They see themselves simply as historians and, if pressed, describe themselves as both humanists and social scientists. They would be reluctant to give up the strengths and advantages of either affiliation; and the fact is that their work presents the same mixture of approaches. Some would say that this ambivalence is just what one would expect of a discipline in transition, or of scholars in transition, from one mode to another. Others would argue that the ambivalence is inherent in the subject matter: some problems lend themselves to one approach; others to the other.

Be that as it may, it would be useful for the purpose of the present inquiry to define our terms, and the clearest way to do this is to present the social science and humanist modes as ideal types at opposite poles of the spectrum of methodology. This does violence to the real character of historians and the history they write: historians are typically men of caution and moderation who do their best to avoid extremes. Still, if we keep in mind that the antinomies that follow are a heuristic device, a figment, they will help clarify the divisions within the historical profession and the problems confronted by social science history as one of several complementary, yet often competing, approaches to the subject.

THE DEFINITION OF THE WORK:
GENERAL VERSUS UNIQUE,
ABSTRACT VERSUS COMPLEX

1. a. The social science approach is problem-oriented. It assumes that there are uniformities of human behavior that transcend time and place and can be studied as such; and the historian as social scientist chooses his problems with an eye to discovering, verifying, or illuminating such uniformities. The aim is to produce general statements of sufficiently specific content to permit analogy and prediction.

[1] Charles J. Erasmus and Waldemar R. Smith, "Cultural Anthropology in the United States since 1900: A Quantitative Analysis," *Southwestern Journal of Anthropology*, XXIII (1967), 111–40.

1. b. The humanist views any such extraction of human experience from its matrix of time and place as an insult to the integrity of the historical process. He feels that human beings and their life in society are far too complex to be simplified in this manner; and without simplification, there is no generalization. As Isaiah Berlin has said, it is the job of a science to concentrate on similarities; whereas the historian is interested in what differentiates. The effort to abstract generalizations, "if it were feasible [and Berlin clearly has his doubts], would be the task of sociology, which would then stand to history as a 'pure' science to its application." [2]

Many historians, moreover, would argue that complexity, far from being a disadvantage, is a source of intellectual pleasure and stimulation. Again, to quote Isaiah Berlin:

> If we ask ourselves what historians have commanded the most lasting admiration, we shall, I think, find that they are neither the most ingenious, nor the most precise, nor even the discoverers of new facts or causal connections, but those who (like imaginative writers) present men or societies or situations in many dimensions, at many interesting levels simultaneously, writers in whose accounts human lives, and their relations both to each other and to the external world, are what (at our most lucid and imaginative) we know that they can be (p. 31).

METHOD: SYSTEM VERSUS ART

2. a. In his effort to derive generalizations that will fit into the larger corpus of social and behavioral science, the historian as social scientist aims self-consciously at methodological rigor. He defines his terms, states his hypothesis, clarifies his assumptions (in so far as he himself is aware of them), and stipulates the criteria of proof. If possible—and for the moment this is largely confined to a field like economic history—he states his hypothesis in the form of an explanatory model, preferably in mathematical language and so framed that the criteria of proof are measurable.

2. b. The historian as humanist has no need of this elaborate

procedure (though he would pretend to no less methodological rigor). Since he starts with the subject rather than with a question, he often does not begin with a preliminary hypothesis. Rather he derives his conclusions in the course of research and then writes his story in accordance with the evidence, framing the exposition in such a way as to convey his interpretation and the reasons for it. Even if he does begin with a hypothesis, he prefers to avoid what he believes to be the literary infelicities inherent in the elaboration of an explicit model. His primary concern remains the story, and he prefers to weave his assumptions and interpretations into the account in such a way as not to detract from its fluency and interest. In general, he prizes subtlety more than precision.

QUANTIFICATION: PRO AND CON

3. a. These differences in approach show up perhaps most clearly in the use and treatment of numerical concepts. Both kinds of historian use such concepts, though the humanist is sometimes not aware of the quantitative implications of such words as "usually," "many," "most of," "often," and the like. The historian as social scientist is keen to measure, and although he would not go so far as to say that only what can be measured is science, he would argue (or at least some would argue) that some number, however approximate, is better than no number—so long as one has some notion of the range of error.

3. b. The historian as humanist is, first of all, skeptical: he knows that many aspects of human behavior are simply not reducible to numbers; and knowing the credence that readers are liable to give to anything that gives the appearance of precision, he prefers no number to what he feels is the spurious assurance of an approximate number. Secondly, his preoccupation with the personages of his story, his concern for their individuality, his effort to accomplish an empathic migration and put himself in their place—all these make him hostile to anything that reduces his subjects to digits. Numbers constitute an artificial normalization of selected characteristics of intrinsically unique persons or events; hence they dehumanize.

No issue dividing humanists and social-scientific historians arouses more emotion than this one. The quantifiers bring to their case a zeal and conviction bordering on arrogance. Edward Kirkland, an economic historian of an older, humanistic tradition, described a book by Robert Fogel, one of the most passionate and militant representatives of the New Economic History, as follows:

> In essence this volume is a new manifesto which, if I get the message, threatens: "retool, rethink, conform, or be plowed under." New are the assumption of infallibility, the all-or-nothing tone, the disdain for words and style, by inference a means of making error plausible. Every page, give or take fifteen, has a statistic but never a trace (beware the implicit quantification!) of humor about either themselves or those who differ from them. In my estimation this approach is not well designed to win friends or influence people or to further interdisciplinary cooperation, which the new breed also advocates.[3]

If Kirkland is sarcastic, Carl Bridenbaugh is shrill, warning the historian never to "worship at the shrine of that Bitch-goddess, QUANTIFICATION," [4] and Arthur Schlesinger, Jr., is counterdogmatic. To those who regard as significant only what is measurable, he retorts: "As a humanist, I am bound to reply that almost all important questions are important precisely because they are not susceptible to quantitative answers." [5]

ESTHETICS

4. a. The disagreement about numbers is related to a difference in esthetic priorities. The historian as social scientist knows that tables of statistics do not scan well. They break the rhythm of the text, and comments on numerical matters are often tedious in their factuality. Still, he is reconciled to these failings. His primary virtues are clarity, precision, and analytical rigor. Besides, some subjects simply do not lend themselves to dramatic or elegant presentation.

4. b. The historian as humanist cherishes the ideal of history as literature. He wants to be an artist as well as a scholar. Style, pace,

---

[3] Edward Kirkland, review of Robert Fogel, *Railroads and American Economic Growth*, in *American Historical Review*, LXXII (July, 1967), 1494f.

[4] Carl Bridenbaugh, "The Great Mutation," *American Historical Review*, LXVIII (January, 1963), 326.

[5] Arthur Schlesinger, Jr., "The Humanist Looks at Empirical Social Research," *American Sociological Review*, XXVI (December, 1961), 770.

and elegance are important, and even ambiguity may be cultivated for its power to stimulate thought. As for numbers, there are humanists who would confine them to pagination; they break the rhythm of the prose.

These are the antitypes and, like all such ideal versions of a diversity of specimens, they verge on caricature. Most historians, we have noted, fall somewhere in between, combining in their work and intellectual stance elements of both schools. What is more, the social sciences–humanities dichotomy is only one of several divisions within the profession. There are those who are drawn to history primarily by a psychological affinity for distant times and places, and those who want to understand their own time or the nature of change through time. Similarly, there are those who seek, however vainly, the ideal of an objective truth (all the social-scientific historians would presumably be included in this camp); while others, as we have seen, deny the existence of this objective, autonomous truth and insist that history is a subjective perception of the historian, who inevitably alters his subject in the course of studying it.

Among these, some look upon subjectivity not as a handicap but as an opportunity. Since history, in their view, is not "what really was," but what the historian says it was, the great historian is the one who shapes our history for us. He may shape it, as Jules Michelet or Henry Adams tried to do, in accordance with his own great vision.[6] Or he may shape it, as many political radicals would do today, as an instrument of change. We are living in an age that is beginning to fear and mistrust science and technology, that wants to substitute heart for mind, warmth for coolness, passion for reason. The committed activist historian joins here with outsiders who have no patience with professional canons and inhibitions. At the 1969 meetings of the American Council on Education, John Monro, former dean of Harvard College and then director of freshman studies at Miles College, denounced a scholar who had called for "a careful, balanced approach to black history." Monro said: "I wonder how much respect we can have for 'academic history' in a day when we discover that for decade after dangerous decade, as tensions mounted toward revolution in our society, our professional academic historians really could not see the importance of Negro history. . . .

[6] See Alfred Kazin, "History and Henry Adams," *The New York Review of Books* (October 23, 1969), p. 24.

Too much of the jam we are now in as a nation grows out of the cool, blind prejudices of our professional historians." [7]

The point of view expressed by Mr. Monro is characteristic of an increasingly vociferous assault on "ivory-tower scholarship." Many students, and some professional historians, have begun to argue that history as conventionally practiced is either a waste of time or a tool of oppression. The attack is directed against all historical work that claims or tries to be scientific and disinterested, but focuses with special sharpness on quantitative work, precisely because it embodies better than any other kind of history the pretensions and aspirations of the historian as scientist.

The experienced quantitative historian is perfectly aware that figures can be made to lie and that sloppy measurements or careless numerical reasoning can lead to erroneous conclusions. But he sees three advantages to quantitative data:

1. The mathematical representation of arguments and the quantitative matching of theory with data require the historian to state his assumptions clearly, to follow out his reasoning step by step, and to face the possibility of refutation; they keep him honest.

2. The assembly of quantitative data makes it less likely that the historian will respond to the odd, unusual case and more likely that he will instead observe the whole sweep of change and the whole character of contrast between different periods, places, or groups of people.

3. The quantitative idiom and the open presentation of quantitative evidence makes it more likely that other students of the same subject will be able to verify, modify, or refute the conclusions the original investigator has drawn from his data. Reliance on quantitative data is thus a protection against the distortions of accident or of personal or ideological bias, which have freer rein in more intuitive or qualitative work.

Some radical historians, like some radical economists or sociologists, reject this belief, not only on the ground that all historians are biased whatever their technique, but also on the ground that quantitative history (like econometrics) embodies a particularly subtle and pernicious form of conservative bias. First, they would argue that the concentration on numerical data, especially on aggregates

[7] Boston *Globe* (October 13, 1969), p. 46.

and averages, tends to dehumanize and sterilize problems, masking the record of man's inhumanity to man under a swarm of anodyne digits. Furthermore it is precisely the apparent objectivity of numbers that makes them so dangerous in the eyes of some of the new-style radicals. Reliance on quantification, in this view, entails both mystification and an evasion of the responsibility to relate one's work to one's political and moral position and to persuade others through that work.

At the extreme this argument comes to a fundamentally subjectivist position: There is no objective truth; each historian brings his biases with him and writes biased history; all efforts to suppress or minimize these biases are bound to fail; hence there is no point in trying to write objective history; indeed every such effort is a mystification. Rather, each historian must write his own history, whose virtue lies in its political impact.

A variant of this position is a reaffirmation of the ethnic basis of scholarship—not generally, perhaps, but for those areas of research and teaching that treat the experience of minority groups or non-white peoples. Because of the inherent subjectivity of history, the argument runs, and indeed of all social science, the scholar's range of empathy and comprehension is necessarily confined to those aspects of his subject that he can claim to feel and understand through inheritance and experience. Only a black can know what it is like to be black. Hence, only a black can write the history of blacks.

Finally, there is a sociopolitical basis for the hostility of some of the New Left to quantitative history and social science. The techniques required to process and analyze numerical data are often complicated and esoteric. They are not easy to learn and constitute in themselves both a diversion from the "real task" of the historian and a filter that excludes those would-be historians (or economists or sociologists) who possess the requisite "understanding" (that is, whose hearts are in the right place) but lack the time, inclination, or talent for quantification. What is more, in so far as quantitative data are stored and used in machine-readable form, they are not accessible in the sense that book knowledge is accessible. It takes money to use a computer. This differential access, some radical students have contended, favors the rich against the poor, the "establishment" against the oppressed, the more so as much of this knowledge may in fact be useful in the maintenance of the status quo against the forces of change. Hence, runs the argument, we should not be seeking and accumulating this form of knowledge.

This critique has some strong points. It calls attention to the frequency with which men have used, and misused, historical arguments to further some particular belief or program of action. (That, of course, is a criticism that cuts two ways.) It blows the dust off long-neglected questions concerning the nature of historical knowledge. Its proponents have identified neglected problems and suggested new interpretations of such institutions as slavery, the factory, and the modern state. All these contributions are welcome.

The danger lies in the conversion of a critique into an ideology. The logic of the extreme subjectivist position seems to rest either on the idea that if all objects are somehow flawed, there is no way to say which ones are more flawed than the others, that is, that *all* reality is ultimately unknowable; or that there is something peculiar about human nature (and therefore human history) that makes it impossible to understand in any reliable way. If either of these arguments were true, it would render useless not only historical study, but also any inquiry into the human condition.

We reject this nihilism. We also reject the "activist" attack on so-called "ivory-tower scholarship." It takes more arrogance than we can muster to impose a set political task on a whole body of knowledge. As the last few decades have shown very clearly, political priorities change fast . . . and historical knowledge accumulates slowly. To commit historians to the exclusive pursuit of this year's or even this generation's political problems (as interpreted by self-appointed censors) would condemn them to intellectual servitude and uselessness. And it would stifle the innovative and even revolutionary consequences of knowledge pursued for its own sake.

Let us sum up our position on these complicated and controversial questions with three straightforward statements:

1. The inability of the historian to shed his biases entirely does not justify the abandonment of all efforts to surmount or minimize the biases in the search for truth and objectivity. The goal may be finally unattainable, but we will never get closer to it if we do not strive for it. Some historians do in fact come closer to it than others. Some history is more objective and less biased, better documented and more cogently argued. Most of us would call that better history.

2. Ethnic criteria of the validity of historical research and teaching are unacceptable because they are anti-intellectual. It may well be that some things are knowable only to "insiders"; but then there are other things that are especially perceptible to "outsiders" pre-

cisely because they are outside. That is one of the ambiguities of historical research: the scholar tries to get as close to his subject as possible while maintaining enough distance of space and time to afford him a sense of context and significance.

3. The validity of any technique of inquiry is not its accessibility but its effectiveness. The answer to inequality of access to knowledge is equality of access, not less knowledge. As for those inequalities that arise from differences in personal talent or predilection, the answer lies once again in freedom and diversity of approach, not in the discouragement or suppression of any particular approach.

In the light of this diversity of approaches, two questions suggest themselves:

1. Is there a historical discipline, in the sense of a branch of knowledge based on common standards of inquiry and dealing with a common subject in a characteristic way?
2. What are the prospects of history as social science?

There are those who would answer the first question in the negative. George H. Nadel, editor of *History and Theory*, announced a conference on "History and Social Science" as follows:

> The opening up of new lines of historical inquiry and the development of new techniques of research (many of them borrowed from the social sciences) have gone so far that it is doubtful whether the notion of "history" as a discipline has any core meaning at all, so various are the meanings that can be imputed to it.[8]

This is too negative. Historians of all stripes do have two things in common: the assumption, first, that the present is the child of the past and that nothing is understandable except as seen through time; and second, that the truth is always complex. The first may seem banal or trivial—the kind of principle that anyone in any discipline would be prepared to subscribe to. And indeed, scholars in other disciplines often do preface their studies of a given problem with a consideration of antecedents, and an increasing number are undertaking research that is exclusively historical in character. In

[8] Cited by C. Vann Woodward, "History and the Third Culture," *Journal of Contemporary History*, III (1969), 24.

that, they are behaving as historians. Still, there are abiding differences of emphasis and degree. Other disciplines are far more ready to build an analysis on the evidence of a moment or a short period. The historian's minimal interval of understanding is longer.

By the same token, other disciplines are prepared to build more with less, to rest more on less, than the historian. They understand and have come to terms with the need to abstract and simplify: as an economist once put it, one good reason is enough. Another economist—a very young one, admittedly—once prefaced a talk on the Industrial Revolution as follows:

> Economic historians have always tended to see the Industrial Revolution as the product of a conjuncture of factors. I have always been dissatisfied with this approach and have been convinced that there is one element that sets everything else in motion. That's what I want to talk about tonight.

Historians, even those historians who want to be social scientists, find this happy simplicity hard to take.

These twin beacons of doctrine illuminate in turn a whole range of other characteristics of the historical profession. Because of the historian's concern with a past that is at once infinitely complex and at best imperfectly known, because he must rely on sources that are always incomplete and often sparse, he has come to place enormous emphasis on the techniques of gathering and evaluating evidence. No profession has set greater store by data—all kinds of data, big, small, important, trivial. Every little bit counts. Hence the respect of the historian for erudition—for the ubiquitous footnote, for the obscure reference, for the long array of variant texts. Hence also the goal of the definitive work, which is not the last word in interpretation (that, never!) but the last word in research: every conceivable source has been consulted. There is no doctrine of diminishing returns, no significance principle (what difference would it make if such and such a source were not taken into account?). The force of this doctrine varies, to be sure, from one branch of the discipline to another and from one country to another. (In France, where completeness of documentation is a dogma, a professor has been known to conceal a potential source from his own student in order to embarrass him later on the defence of his thesis.) Nevertheless it remains strong, and only the explosive increase in source material, hence the manifest impossibility of reading everything on any subject of scope and significance, is finally eroding the old faith.

Along with this striving for exhaustiveness has gone an inordinate respect for what is called original research—which is not so much research based on original ideas as first-hand research based on personal investigation of the original (that is, primary) sources. Here history seems to be different from other disciplines, whose members are not only pleased to rely on the evidence assembled by others but also base much of their technique of inquiry on the assumption that processed data are available and usable. The historian who is confronted with official statistics, for example, worries a great deal about how the statistics were collected. The economist (not the economic historian) takes them for what they are worth and tries to manipulate them in such a way as to compensate for error. The difference in attitudes shows up clearly in the response to some of the new bibliographical services now becoming available. Whereas most social scientists have accepted with alacrity the opportunity to rely on abstracts for information about current publications, historians have remained suspicious. They look upon this kind of second-hand information as potentially misleading and reliance thereon as a kind of abdication of responsibility. Thus in a report on *Bibliography and the Historian*, Dagmar Perman cites some of the replies to a questionnaire sent by the Joint Committee on Bibliographical Services to History to a random sample of three hundred members of the American Historical Association (only fifty replies were received). The responses were as interesting for what was not wanted as for what was: very few requested further annotation of bibliographical entries and almost none wanted evaluations of these entries; on the contrary, many explicitly stated that they did not consider such evaluations as desirable or useful. This was the respondents' attitude toward publications in their own field. Very few had any interest in bibliographical information on other fields, but paradoxically, in so far as they did want it, they wanted carefully selected, highly annotated and evaluative lists.[9]

By the same token, most historians are reluctant to make use of research assistants for any but the most routine tasks or to accept the principle of group research, in which responsibilities are divided and each member does, and hence by historical standards knows,

[9] Dagmar H. Perman, ed., *Bibliography and the Historian: The Conference at Belmont of the Joint Committee on Bibliographical Services to History, May 1967* (Santa Barbara, Calif.: 1968), pp. 7–19.

only a piece of the whole. It is not only that the historian rarely has the funds to pay an assistant or that historians would find it difficult to finance a large-scale group project. The point is that so long as historiography is seen as an art as well as a branch of knowledge, historical work becomes an intensely personal thing and hence indivisible and noninterchangeable.

This point of view has interesting consequences for the historian's attitude toward research as an activity competing with other activities for scarce time. If the product of research is personal, it is not necessarily cumulative or additive; some research is worth doing because of the subject and the person doing it, but much work is a waste of time, the researcher's and the readers'. Hence the remark of one respondent to our Special Survey of Historians: "We need Malthusian restraint in research, *not* expansion, support, or encouragement. Demand quality and accept no substitutes." For similar reasons, historians are often suspicious of courses in methodology and hostile to any kind of normalization of research procedure. If historiography is art, it cannot and must not be reduced to some kind of routine. It is almost as though some scholars felt that historians are born, not made. To quote the same respondent in regard to the desirability of retooling historians to understand and utilize new techniques: "He should be a self-stropping blade to start with. Nothing makes up for a dull edge at any time after that." Some respondents even resented the use of a word like "retooling." [10] "What does this mean?" wrote one. "My tools are my head and a pencil." (The same person wrote that he thought of himself as a humanist only. "I consider the social sciences to be pseudosciences, like alchemy and astrology.") Another recoiled with almost palpable distaste: "This is a horrid word! Why not 'retooling in depth'!"

[10] In this regard, the historian stands somewhere between the pure social scientist and the pure humanist. At an *"Ad Hoc* meeting on the Humanities" sponsored by the Office of Scientific Personnel of the National Research Council as part of a larger Study of Postdoctoral Education in the United States (June 10, 1968), half those present found occasion to vent their suspicion of or hostility to research. One participant began by asking why it was necessary to publish doctoral theses. Some of the best work in creative writing, he noted, was never published; some of the most original musical compositions were never played. Maybe, he went on, we ought to celebrate the burning of the great library in Alexandria (here he lost his classicist confreres); we have too much to read already. Postdoctoral research, he thought, ought to be restricted to special cases. This was a sentiment that encountered wide approval. Where would we be if all faculty members in the humanities were engaged in research? asked another. And still another volunteered that even the notion of research embodies a model that gets in our way.

These values have, to be sure, a strong intellectual justification. In so far as history attempts to see things whole, it is, more than other disciplines, dependent on individual perceptions. Interpretation and understanding are never routine; there are too many variables to reduce the analysis to some kind of procedure. Hence it is important that each scholar dig down to bedrock. He comes with new questions and concepts to old material as well as new; and if he permits himself to rely entirely on the ruminations of others, he has given half the game away.

It is one thing to justify this attitude in principle, however, and another to establish it as a moral absolute. Nothing comes free, and the insistence on "original" research is bought at a price. No other discipline builds so slowly, because the members of no other discipline are so reluctant as historians to stand on the shoulders of others. All historians can recall criticisms of colleagues and students on the ground that their work was too derivative at one point or another, that it relied too heavily on secondary sources. In one such discussion a man's job hung in the balance . . . until one scholar observed: "Why not? I always thought I was writing these monographs so that someone else could use them."

2
THE PROFESSION OF
HISTORY IN THE
UNITED STATES

It is against this background of the intellectual characteristics of the historical profession that its material circumstances are best understood.

To begin with, there is the question of numbers: historians constitute a large and rapidly growing group. If all those who teach history at any level were counted, plus those amateurs who contribute to historical knowledge on an antiquarian level, we would arrive at a number in five figures. Even if the group is confined to those teaching and doing research at the university level—as it is in this report—the number reaches the thousands. Membership in the American Historical Association, which does not include all historians in universities but does include numerous others (those in institutions, teachers in elementary and secondary schools, and amateurs), was 19,037 at the end of 1968. Only psychology and economics, of the other behavioral and social sciences, had more members in their associations, and the Historical Association was growing at that time more rapidly than the others. In the eleven years from 1957 to 1968, membership had more than tripled, as against a doubling in economics and political science, and an increase of two thirds in psychology.

This growth has been proportional to the increase in output of undergraduates concentrating in history: 11,692 BA's in 1957; 31,793 in 1967. By comparison, the increase in the number of history MA's has been even more rapid: 1,256 in 1957 and 4,621 in 1967. The number of PhD's has gone up more slowly: 314 in 1957; 655 a decade later. These data would seem to indicate that the determining factor in the expansion of the profession has been the demand for

22

teaching personnel; unlike the practitioners of the other behavioral and social sciences, historians are not the beneficiaries of a specific demand for their services from outside the academy. There is, to be sure, some employment of house historians by corporate institutions, public and private; and certain fields of government service—military and political intelligence, for example—have found the critical faculties and perceptions developed by a profession that habitually works with incomplete information to be ideally suited to their needs. But these employments are exceptional and constitute only a small fraction of the discipline.

These are the latest aggregate data available. Projections based on these indicate that the number of BA's will rise to 91,000 by 1977, the number of MA's to 15,000, and the number of PhD's to 1,600.[1] More recent partial returns, however, indicate that this expansion may be over; indeed, that there may be a contraction of the profession in the immediate future. In the last two academic years (1968–69 and 1969–70) the number of students in history courses and the number of students concentrating on history have leveled off and turned downward, with immediate repercussions on the demand for graduate teaching assistants and eventual effects—if the drop persists—on the demand for regular instructors.

It is somewhat early to analyze this abrupt change of trend, but one factor often adduced is a growing feeling, alluded to above, that history is not "relevant." It deals with the past, and students are concerned with the present and future. Besides, the study of history implies that we can learn from the past, that is, from experience, and this runs counter to widespread convictions among the young that (1) they face unprecedented problems for which experience offers no guide; (2) that their elders have given enough proof of their incompetence to disqualify themselves as experts; and (3) that the record of man's frustrated aspirations and his inhumanity to his fellow man is so discouraging that history is in its essence the "wet blanket" of the social sciences. (The effort of some radical historians to produce a politically "justifiable" kind of history—"from the bottom up"—is in part, no doubt, a response to this indictment.) By comparison, fields like sociology and government, present-minded and strongly oriented toward policy-making and social engineering, are far more attractive.

Such fluctuations in student demand have occurred before and

[1] *The Behavioral and Social Sciences: Outlook and Needs* (Englewood Cliffs, N. J.: Prentice-Hall, Inc., 1969), Appendix D.

will presumably happen again. It would be a mistake for history to ignore the present trend, insofar as it implies a criticism of the present range of course offerings. It would be an even more serious mistake to cater to the trend at the sacrifice of those standards of inquiry and instruction that are the foundation of the discipline or at the neglect of lines of research that may be less "relevant" today but are of enduring concern to scholarship.

Affluence and numbers rarely coincide. By comparison with the other behavioral and social sciences, history is a poor relation. It receives its share of university funds because of its instructional responsibilities; other things being equal, such funds tend, over time, to be allocated in proportion to the number of students taught and similar criteria. But it receives only a pittance from outside sources, which are channeled overwhelmingly, first, to the natural sciences, then to the more "scientific" and equipment-using of the behavioral and social sciences. This relative impoverishment shows up in all the statistical data. The annual operating costs per full-time equivalent faculty member of PhD-granting history departments came to $15,230 in 1967; the most favored of the social sciences, psychology, spent $24,020; the mean of six social sciences was $18,750.[2] Whereas the average large psychology department was using equipment valued at $448,120, and the average large department even in less experimental disciplines like economics and sociology enjoyed a capital stock of $13,820 and $31,050 respectively, history could draw on a modest pool of typewriters and ditto machines, plus an occasional adding machine, valued at an average of $2,350 per PhD-granting department. The major psychology departments averaged 1,263 square feet of space per faculty member; the mean for the social sciences was 565 square feet; history, as usual at the bottom of the list, enjoyed 227 square feet. What is more, these departmental figures are only a partial indication of the discrepancy between history and the other disciplines; for in the other social sciences, far more than in history, much of the research is undertaken in institutes and centers independent of university departments. These have their own plants, their own budgets, their own offices: in 1966 they accounted for 35 percent of research expenditures in the social and behavioral sciences (as against 34 percent for departments and 31 percent for professional schools). Most of these institutes, to be sure, are interdisciplinary in character and a number have found places for historians

[2] The six disciplines are anthropology, economics, history, political science, psychology, and sociology.

on their staff; but these are a small privileged group and account for a small fraction of these research outlays and facilities.[3]

Spelled out in real terms, this means that the historian—even the elder statesman of established scholarly reputation—rarely receives summer support or has an assistant or secretary of his own; that his department is drastically underequipped with microfilm readers, duplication and photo reproduction equipment, recording equipment, and the other tools of his trade; that he lacks the office space and spatial arrangements most conducive to effective teaching and research; and that he cannot afford the travel and telephonic communications that have made it possible in other disciplines, particularly the natural sciences, to talk of an international community of scholars. The one really costly installation used and considered indispensable by historians—for the modesty of their circumstances is matched by the modesty of their expectations—is the library; but here, as we shall see in Chapter 7, the exponential increase in the volume and cost of new publications has compelled even the greatest libraries to sacrifice the quality and accessibility of their collections, while the growing dependence of the other social sciences on forms of reading matter and evidential material other than books has left historians almost alone (except for allies from literature and the other humanities) in their efforts to persuade university authorities to put more money into libraries.

This condition of relative deprivation varies, to be sure, from one school to another. Generally speaking, the larger and wealthier the college or university, the higher the salaries, the lighter the teaching load (especially in the early years), the more generous the leave policy, and the better the facilities for research. The variation in these respects can be very large, ranging from as many as five preparations a week in some schools to two or even one in some terms in the stronger institutions.

The correlation between strength and wealth on the one hand and opportunities for research on the other is not a smooth one: the oldest and most prestigious of the private institutions have been far slower than the state universities to create research professorships or make half-time teaching appointments, on the ground that these represent a tacit erosion of the teaching function. The private institutions, moreover, perhaps because of their smaller size, have been less willing to single out certain men for special treatment.

[3] *The Behavioral and Social Sciences: Outlook and Needs*, Tables 10-1, 10-4, 10-7, and 10-9, pp. 156, 162, 168–69, and 172–73, respectively.

In general, however, the rule is that the rich get richer, that is, have more time to work, publish, and win fame; and the poor have more classes.

Insofar as the historian tries to eke out his income by writing, he does potboilers (the name is suggestive of their purpose) for newspapers and magazines or textbooks of one kind or another. In fairness, one should not scorn either of these activities. On the one hand, one of the functions of the historical profession is to communicate with the larger public; on the other, a good textbook is the best way for a first-class scholar to reach and teach the greatest number of students. Unfortunately, the understandable desire of historians for additional income is an encouragement to overeager publishers who see each book as a possible gold mine or, at worst, a vein withheld from competitors; so that there are far too many texts published, to say nothing of those that never appear but keep their authors busy for years and years. Many of these scholars could presumably use this time to the advancement of knowledge; and while some might argue that there is already too much published in guise of scholarship (which sometimes simply means that there is too much for some people to keep up with), one might reasonably expect that sufficient and selective financial support for research would go a long way toward fructifying the labor thus released. In any event, it should be noted that the scientific productivity of the discipline is adversely affected by its relative penury—and more and more so as historians try to keep up with the Joneses in other, more favored, disciplines.

This is the heart of the matter: the comparison, first, with what already exists in other disciplines; and second with what might and should be in history. It would not be hard to show, for example, that American historians are better off than those of other lands; or that American historians of today are better equipped and financed than their teachers were. But these arguments are beside the point; and coming, as they sometimes do, from scholars who have the good fortune to teach and work in the richest departments, they are complacent and condescending—like the consolation sometimes offered Afro-Americans when they are told that they are richer than most people in other parts of the world and better off than their ancestors.

Does this picture of the historical profession seem exaggerated? What do individual historians say about their conditions? To get some idea, we went out and asked them.

In April and May, 1968, the History Panel mailed out a short questionnaire to about 1,000 regular members of the history departments of twenty-nine American colleges and universities. Over the next six weeks, roughly 600 of those historians sent back usable questionnaires, 40 sent word of their refusal or inability to answer, 100 sent some other form of reply, and 260 did not respond at all. The list of departments intentionally emphasized large, prestigious graduate departments, but it also included six good institutions doing little or no training of graduate students in history. Altogether, the twenty-nine departments gave 64 percent of the PhD's in history granted in the United States from 1960 to 1966. The sample therefore gives a fairly good picture of what is going on in the institutions giving the bulk of American historians their advanced training, even if it seriously underrepresents the smaller and less prestigious departments.

The topographic map of the profession that emerges shows a rough, uneven terrain. Four fundamental features show up in the data:

1. a rather unequal distribution of historical specialties among different sorts of departments and academic positions.
2. a wide variation in research interests, needs, and support according to special field, type of institution, and position within the institution.
3. a standard life cycle of research experience.
4. some change in these matters from one generation of historians to the next.

Let us take each of these up briefly, in turn.

Within the sample, African and Asian historians are disproportionately concentrated in the highest-prestige institutions, West European historians in the smaller liberal arts colleges, intellectual historians in both rather than in the departments of middling reputation. Within their institutions, historians of Asia, Africa, and Eastern Europe had affiliations with research centers fairly frequently, while historians of the United States or Western Europe rarely had them. Yet it is the historians of the United States and Western Europe who include the highest proportions of full professors, while the newer fields of East European, Asian, African, and Latin American history include many junior men. Likewise, diplomatic historians, economic historians, and, most notably, the much younger group of historians of science concentrate in the senior ranks, while political, social, and intellectual historians occupy the junior positions. These variations show up as substantial percentage differences.

TABLE 2-1   DISTRIBUTION OF HISTORIANS BY SPECIALTY

Specialty	Number	Percentage Who Are Full Professors	Percentage Who Are Assistant Professors or Below
Diplomatic history	55	66%	18%
Economic history	44	64	16
History of science	18	50	33
Intellectual history	79	46	33
Political history	119	42	34
None given	46	41	28
Social history	99	37	31
Other specialties	123	62	13
Total	583	50%	26%

Source: Special survey of historians in twenty-nine history departments (see Appendix B).

All this means that an economic historian of Asia (to take an extreme case) is quite likely to hold senior appointments in both a department of history and a research center within a high-prestige institution and a historian of European science a similar position without the center affiliation, while the odds are better that an American political historian will hold high rank, without research appointment, in a less distinguished institution and a Latin American social historian a similar appointment at a lower rank. Since rank, quality of institution, and research affiliation all affect the historian's ability to get his work done, the problems faced by members of the various special fields differ considerably.

There are, for example, marked variations in research funds. Figure 2-1, which deals with funds received from outside the university between 1964 and 1967, gives one indication.

Except for the history of science (which is the best-supported field in almost every respect), the specialties receiving heavier outside support are generally those which involve their practitioners in the behavioral and social sciences and which frequently appear in interdisciplinary research centers. Geographically, historians of Latin America, Africa, and Asia do best. That is partly because such people are more likely to undertake expensive forms of research in the first place; it is also because more money is available for research on exotic areas or in interdisciplinary fields like economic history. Over and above these differences by field, our data show the decided advantage (not only in outside grants, but also in university support, teaching load, and released time for research) of the historian in a high-prestige institution or with a research appointment.

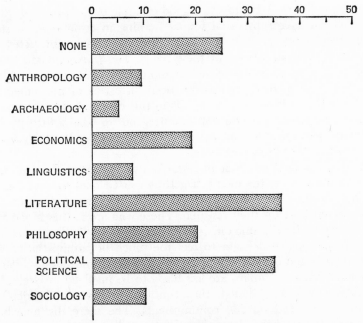

FIGURE 2-1   SPECIAL HISTORY SURVEY: OUTSIDE FUNDS RECEIVED, 1964–1967, BY FIELD

Data from Special Survey of Historians (see Appendix B).

On the whole, with the exception of historians of science, the kinds of historians who are best supported also show the closest tie to the behavioral and social sciences. About a tenth of the historians in the sample have undergraduate degrees in behavioral and social science fields other than history; around 7 percent have PhD's in those fields; and roughly a third claim "substantial training" in at least one of them. About three quarters of the historians queried said that at least one social science field was "particularly important" to their own fields of interest, about two thirds expressed interest in a social science summer training institute, and just over half would choose a social science field for a full year's additional training. Distinguishing between fields, we find that we can divide our historians into three categories: *uninterested, involved,* and *frustrated.* Historians of science and intellectual historians, especially those dealing with Europe and North America, typify those with little social science training, little current contact with these fields, and little desire to change in this regard. Economic historians of the United States, Latin America, or Asia provide a good example of the *involved*: they are likely to have substantial formal training in economics, to stay in contact with economics and economists, and to be interested in extending their knowledge of these fields. The *frustrated* are those with little previous social science training who have come to think that it is vital to their own work: social historians of the Americas tend to fall into this category. While in this case everything depends on the definitions, it would not be outrageous to label a fifth of the historians answering our survey *uninterested*, another third *involved*, and nearly half of them *frustrated*.

A fairly standard life cycle of research also appears in the findings. Within the sample, the men just getting started tend to have heavy teaching loads, course assignments alien to their research interests, and poor support for their research. Those who are farther along begin to acquire funds, time off, and greater control over their teaching assignments, but also begin to feel the pinch of administrative responsibilities and outside commitments to writing and public service. The most senior historians are less likely to be involved in large and expensive research, although they continue to bear the burden of administrative and outside commitments. The more distinguished the institution and the closer the affiliation with a research institute, the earlier the historian achieves the perquisites of seniority.

Finally, some features of the historical landscape are changing with time. Judging by age, year of PhD, or academic rank, we find senior historians concentrated in the traditional fields of North American and West European history (especially diplomatic, intellectual, and political history), with junior men in the newer specialties of East European, African, Asian, and Latin American history. These latter fields include very few people who earned PhD's before 1945. In recent years, Eastern Europe appears to have lost favor, but the others all have more than their share of PhD's earned since 1962. So the very fields which involve their practitioners most heavily in the behavioral and social sciences are the ones which are growing and are currently staffed with junior men.

These younger men have a different outlook on their profession. In answer to our (leading) question, "Do you think of yourself as a social scientist, a humanist, or something of both? Why?" a senior historian at a Midwestern university gave this thoughtful answer, characteristic of the older generation:

> Principally as a humanist because I believe history is principally made of the ideas and actions of men, oftentimes unpredictable, and can not be measured in statistical or "scientific" terms.

One of his more irritable West Coast colleagues added, in capitals:

> THERE IS NO SUCH THING AS A SOCIAL "SCIENCE," ONLY MEN WHO BELIEVE THERE IS ONE.

Another West Coaster replied:

> I do not think of myself as a "social scientist" because (1) I think it a vile term, (2) some of the most fatuous academics I know so proclaim themselves; nor do I think of myself as a "humanist"—although I certainly cherish humanistic values. I am a historian. That is enough of a "little box" for me.[4]

On the other hand, an Asian specialist from the Midwest said:

> I consider myself a social scientist. I was trained as one and view my work as a historian as developing and testing social science theory and method with historical data.

A young historian of Latin America replied flatly: "As a social scientist," but then added this comment on historical method that few humanistic historians would disagree with:

> I do not think that the method is different, but the application of the method by historians certainly differs from that of, for example, sociologists or anthropologists. I think that the historian is generally more penetrating

---

[4] Later, the same writer recommended: "The best thing your committee could possibly do would be to disband without writing a report, let its members get back to productive scholarship, and use the money to benefit some of the less well-funded areas of the profession."

in his search for evidence, and is more rigorous in his application of the method.

The correlation of outlook with age and (more particularly) specialty is strong, if not perfect.

As new fields of inquiry flourish within history, the division of opinion is changing and the genteel poverty of historical researchers may change as well. An increasing number of historians are working in fields that bring them into interdisciplinary research centers and other forms of contact with more favored disciplines. Since they are better financed and better equipped than their fellows, they inevitably produce a kind of demonstration effect among them. (One should not, however, underestimate the significance of an antitechnological backlash among those historians whose interests or temperaments make it difficult or less necessary for them to use the newer techniques or facilities or whose subject areas within the discipline are less favored in this regard. They are tempted to turn privation into an intellectual ideal and to oppose the advantages of others as a source of corruption.)

NEW FORMS OF HISTORICAL WORK

In the meantime, an ever-growing number of schools are experimenting with new programs of interdisciplinary training and research. One evidence is the increased number of courses defined by topic rather than by time and place: the historian is beginning to get away from the conventional boxes and is shaping his materials in new molds. A "Proposal for a Graduate Program in Comparative History at Brandeis University" goes so far as to characterize this shift as reflecting "the advanced thinking of the historical profession, which will shortly be the orthodox form of historiography." "Undergraduates nowadays," it asserts, "are too sophisticated to be excited by the old cliches about the dawn of the modern world in the Renaissance or the making of the French nation: they want history discussed in terms of the political and social categories which they encounter in their courses in the social sciences and which can be illustrated by the patterns of social change the world over." Another is the availability of extradisciplinary options in the choice of fields for the general examination at the conclusion of graduate course work. Still another is the growing number of interdepartmental seminars and courses, often taught by a team of instructors drawn from two or more disciplines. A variation on this theme is the interdisciplinary course for beginning graduate students in history: Princeton's History 500, which introduces the class to readings in political science, sociology, psychology, economics, and other social sciences, while bringing in an array of guest lecturers from appropriate fields, is an excellent example. On the undergraduate level, interdisciplinary training has, if anything, a longer history, with the practice well established of setting minor alongside major subjects and offering special honors programs designed to prevent overspecialization. Moreover, a few schools—Harvard, for example—have introduced concentrations in social studies or social science. All of these arrangements are, needless to say, optional, and some of them owe their considerable success to their selectivity. Only a few of the better students are admitted.

The closest thing to the institutionalization of the social science approach is to be found in a department like that at Pittsburgh, which is not prepared to compete with larger, older departments in across-the-board coverage, but is all the more ready to concentrate its resources on newer approaches to history. Pittsburgh also publishes the *Historical Methods Newsletter,* a quarterly devoted to the *Quantitative Analysis of Social, Economic, and Political Development.* It is no coincidence that the first move to require quantitative training in social science of all undergraduate majors also comes not from one of the high-prestige universities but from the Irvine Campus of the University of California, where all students in these disciplines do two years of mathematics, statistics, and computer science.[5] Nor is it a coincidence that it is the "newer" history departments, those that are not yet major producers of PhD's, that are planning on the largest increases in research equipment over the next decade; it is not that they have less equipment at present than the major departments, but they apparently envisage the needs of instruction and research differently.[6]

---

[5] The historians at Irvine are not subject to these requirements. But the undergraduate program makes a point of shifting the emphasis "from traditional preoccupation with specific countries, areas, and themes (or combination thereof) toward a generic approach" that entails particular attention to methodology and comparative history. The aim is to offer a program of instruction in history as both humanity and social science. Department of History, University of California at Irvine, "Studies in History" (October, 1968).

[6] The large departments valued their equipment in 1967 at an average of $2,350; the others, $2,810. The large departments anticipated needs averaging

The same phenomenon is to be found abroad. In Britain, it is the new universities that have taken the lead in the study of contemporary history, have offered wide geographical coverage, have promoted computer research and similar quantitative excursions, and have sought to concentrate as well as organize their efforts along topical lines (social history, intellectual history, labor history) rather than the conventional chronological and geographical boundaries.[7] The older redbrick universities and, a fortiori, Oxford and Cambridge have been more cautious, but they are following along. Similarly in France, it is the creation of new campuses that is providing opportunities for pedagogical experiment and innovations in research: thus it is the still-unopened campus of Antony that plans to introduce the Irvine formula of math and statistics for all.

The proliferation of new offerings and programs in social-scientific history is evidence of change, and change is a sign of health in any intellectual discipline. It would be a mistake, however, to infer that the historical discipline is going to be taken over by new men using new ways. For at least two generations scholars within and without the discipline have proclaimed the advent of a new era of scientific history, based on the application of quantitative methods and the assimilation of the concepts and theory of the sciences. There has indeed been an important corpus of work along these lines, but insofar as these manifestoes have envisaged a metamorphosis of the discipline and an end to the more traditional kind of history, they have been utterly unrealistic. C. Vann Woodward, remarking on this litany, reminds us of Mark Twain's complaint that the press reports of his death were grossly exaggerated.

$2,000 over the next ten years, the others, $14,000. *The Behavioral and Social Sciences: Outlook and Needs*, Table 10-9, pp. 172–73. The figures in this table suggest some interesting differences between history and the other disciplines in the survey. In every case where there is a significant discrepancy in anticipated needs between "large" and "other" departments, it is the former that have the bigger appetites. Only in political science, always closest to history in relative impoverishment, is the situation reversed as in history. Even in political science, however, anticipated needs of major departments average $11,000, or five times the history figures. Economics estimated, $23,000; sociology, $130,000; and psychology, as always the most costly, $372,000. While it would be too much to say that to him who wants shall be given, one might with reason expect to find some correlation between perceived needs and actual support.
[7] Cf. Brian Harrison, "History at the Universities 1967: A Commentary," *History*, LIII (1968), 357–80; based on G. Barlow, ed., *History at the Universities*, 2nd ed. (London: Historical Association, 1968).

Far from being revolutionized by new techniques, transformed beyond recognition, or swallowed up by the social sciences, much the greater part of history as written in the United States has remained obstinately, almost imperviously traditional. It could be read by historians of the last three generations with scarcely a tremor of surprise over methods and techniques. Like their predecessors and masters, contemporary historians write narrative, largely nonanalytical works. They set great store by working from manuscript sources, verifying the facts, and marshalling the evidence. Their publications are praised or blamed in the professional journals according to the old fashioned canons and values: thoroughness of research, objectivity of view, and clarity of logic, together with lucidity and grace of the writing.[8]

The reason for this conservatism undoubtedly lies in part, as Vann Woodward notes, in the orneriness of human nature. Humanistic historians have felt themselves offended and threatened by the growing interest in the problems and methods of social science and their resentments have been fueled by the "aggressive posture" and "occasional philistinism" of the more zealous adherents of the social science approach. There has been too much trumpeting, often by scholars whose work speaks for itself and needs no advertising. Yet these clashes of temperament and conviction are only surface manifestations of more fundamental difficulties. If history remains a humanistic discipline, it is in large part because its subject matter is man, because many of its most interesting problems do not lend themselves to quantitative, social-scientific treatment, and because many of the recruits to the profession are drawn to it by their affinity for this kind of subject matter and these kinds of problems.

On the other hand, it is obvious that the social science component of history, for all its limitations, is growing, that its techniques, and hence its capabilities, are changing, and that it is developing closer and more effective ties to other disciplines. At the same time, these other disciplines are developing a new interest in history as a storehouse of evidence about human behavior and hence a substitute for the laboratory of the natural scientist. It is often impossible to test

[8] C. Vann Woodward, "History and the Third Culture," *Journal of Contemporary History*, III (1968), 24.

generalizations in social science by replicated experiment, but sometimes history offers sufficient instances for plausible and even persuasive verification and it remains the only window on long-term change. In testimony to this convergence of interest, the number of theses dealing with historical topics has risen sharply in political science and sociology in the last two years (representing the completion of work begun several years earlier) and a growing number of established scholars in these disciplines have brought out works or are engaging in studies of this kind. One thinks of Smelser, Bendix, Lipset, Gusfield, and Moore in sociology—to name only a few; and of Hoffmann, Ullman, and Davies in political science—to say nothing of the many now working in the field of electoral sociology and political behavior on the basis of a growing corpus of machine-readable election data.

Ironically—considering the fuss that is sometimes made—none of this is new. Interdisciplinary history of a quantitative character has a long pedigree. Richard Jensen of Washington University has done a valuable report on "The Development of Quantitative Historiography in America," in which he traces the first serious work along these lines to Francis Walker and the Census Bureau of the 1870s and to the historical seminar of Herbert Baxter Adams and J. Franklin Jameson at the Johns Hopkins University in the 1880s. It was the historians, Jensen points out, who "pioneered the quantitative study of political behavior and social structure in this country." In later years, their role in these domains diminished, in part because the availability of manuscript nonquantitative sources opened new opportunities to them, in part because new kinds of social scientists took over the job. But the tradition is there, and it has received a powerful stimulus in recent years from the availability of new sources (in particular, machine-readable data) and the development in related disciplines of concepts and techniques that make possible a more powerful analysis and more precise evaluation of these and other kinds of historical evidence.

This development is a challenge, but even more, an opportunity. The nature of history is to thrive on diversity. The various approaches nourish and stimulate one another and the inquiries and findings of any one sector are ignored by the others only at their peril. Vann Woodward, speaking for the humanistic point of view, says, "If we can't lick 'em, we must join 'em." There is no question of licking anyone. Historians are united by their common interest in the story of man. The task of the profession—and indeed its virtue —is to learn whatever it has to in order to understand and write that story, and the one thing it cannot afford is a policy of segregation or elitism.

3
VARIETIES OF INTER-DISCIPLINARY AND SOCIAL-SCIENTIFIC HISTORY

It is impossible in short compass to give a comprehensive or balanced picture of contemporary historical scholarship or even of that part of it that comes under the rubric of social science. The range of interest is too wide; the diversity of approach too great. For every person or subject mentioned, many more must necessarily be slighted.

The difficulty is compounded by the nature of the historical inquiry. Because of the incompleteness of the evidence, hence its ambiguities, and because of the complexity of the subject matter, hence its resistance to abstraction, theoretical construction, and generalization, historiography does not show the cumulative progress characteristic of the natural sciences and, in lesser degree, of some of the social and behavioral sciences. The discipline advances partly by the addition of new data or verification of old, partly by reconsideration and reappraisal of old problems in the light of new evidence or new questions. The answers furnished by this process of rumination are not definitive; and because they are subject in their own turn to reexamination, they do not constitute an unambiguous extension of the frontier of knowledge. They are rather an enrichment of the intellectual content of the discipline—something more to chew on and ponder; hence something to bring us closer to the subtle, complex wisdom that is required for an understanding of the subtle, complex problems of the real world.

As in the other social sciences, this process of reexamination is not simply a function of the logic of the inquiry. Invariably it reflects the special problems and interests of the day, partly because scholars, in spite of what students may think, are not immune to considerations of "relevance," partly because university administrations, philanthropic foundations, and public sources of funds are ever responsive to topical concerns and allocate their support accordingly. Each generation, therefore, writes its own history. Two generations ago, in 1931, a conference of American historians summoned by the American Historical Association to consider, among other things, possible avenues for future research, listed as a neglected field the "history of race relations and of race acculturation" and suggested as "sample studies," "The Civilizing of the American Indian" and "The Effect of German Immigration upon Musical Development"—those, and nothing more.[1] We have come a little way since 1931.

One may perhaps best convey this pattern of intellectual development by reviewing the course of the historiography of a given subject: revolution. This is an old and ever-popular theme, because it deals with a particularly crucial and dramatic aspect of power, and history, from its beginnings, has always had a marked predilection for the wielders of power. The earliest treatments of the subject are mingled with chronicles of the acts and vicissitudes of rulers and were usually written to denounce the evil of rebellion or assert the legitimacy of a new line. Not until historians began to look carefully at the great French revolution that ushered in the modern age (the French date what they call *histoire contemporaine* from 1789), did the study of the subject shift from the realm of dramatic or apologetic narrative to serious analysis.

As one might expect, French scholars showed the way, in particular Michelet and Tocqueville. They laid the methodological groundwork in their reliance on manuscript archives and other primary sources at a time when access to and utilization of such recent materials were still rare; and each in his own way showed the power of intellect cum imagination to give meaning to the past. Michelet saw the revolution as the work of the people personified as the nation; no historian or even novelist, save perhaps Carlyle, has better conveyed the drama and passion of those times. Tocqueville was the colder mind, and by studying the sources of the Revolution in the Old Regime, he was able to situate it in the larger context of a half-millennium of nation-building and centralization. The one saw

---

[1] *Historical Scholarship in America: Needs and Opportunities*, A Report by the Committee of the American Historical Association on the Planning of Research (New York, 1932).

the birth of a new era; the other, the consummation of a long effort. They were both right.

In the decades that followed, the French continued to concentrate a substantial portion of their historical research in this area—understandably, for the Revolution was France's coming-of-age and the interpretation of that event was the primary element in France's self-image. Much of the work consisted in filling in the details, but insofar as it aimed at analysis, it sought particularly to understand the causes of the Revolution. Two schools developed: one saw the Revolution as an expression of the frustration of a rising bourgeoisie and a relatively favored peasantry in the face of the burdens and inequities imposed by obsolete institutions; and another saw the uprising as an inevitable consequence of immemorial misery and exploitation brought to a boil by a financial and commercial crisis, itself climaxed by a bad harvest and famine prices. These findings also had relevance for an understanding of the phenomenon of revolution as such, although French scholars were usually unconcerned with the general problem.

The effort to situate the French upheaval in a comparative context has a venerable pedigree, going back to the contemporary writings of Burke and Gentz. Both these men, the Irishman and the Austrian, were conservatives who drew on history to distinguish between good revolutions—for Burke, the "Glorious Revolution" of 1688; for Gentz, the American Revolution—and bad. The bad revolution was the French—bad because it was angry, contemptuous of personal rights, destructive of valuable and valid links to the past.[2] These early essays, obviously, were not studies of revolution for its own sake but invidious comparisons of selected examples for polemical purposes.

The shift from the particular to the general was in large part the work of Marx and Engels, whose preoccupation with the subject was implicit in their political aspirations. They came to the problem with an all-embracing philosophy of history that led them to force the revolutions of the past into schematic categories and misled them about the timing and character of the revolutions of the future. Thus later generations of Marxist historians have had their work

---

[2] Edmund Burke, *Reflections on the Revolution in France* (1790); Friedrich von Gentz, *Origin and Principles of the American Revolution, Compared with the Origin and Principles of the French Revolution*, trans. John Quincy Adams (Philadelphia, 1800). The Gentz essay first appeared in his *Historisches Journal* (Berlin), an antirevolutionary periodical that was subsidized by the British.

cut out for them reconciling theory and facts and settling issues of doctrinal purity. Much of their energy, moreover, has been absorbed by questions of doing rather than knowing: Are revolutions historically predetermined? If so, can the revolutionary sit by and let history provide the occasion? Or should he help history along? If he should help, how does he know when to act? In a society where the state has almost a monopoly of force, when does adventurism become revolution? All of these are questions that have troubled Marxists ever since the bloody June Days of 1848 and they are still to the fore today.

In the meantime, the very process of coming to terms with the Marxist formulation, by both Marxists and non-Marxists, directly and indirectly stimulated research in this area in all the social sciences. Most of this work rested implicitly or explicitly on historical evidence; but the historians themselves were slower to venture on generalizations than sociologists, social psychologists, and political scientists, whose explanatory models made the task of selection and comparison easier and more congenial. Historians who spent a good part of their lives learning to know one revolution well—or one aspect of one revolution—found much of this generalizing superficial in its sweep and erroneous in its details.

It was principally American historians who first ventured into the domain of systematic, inductive comparison. One of the earliest was Crane Brinton, who brought out in 1938 his *Anatomy of Revolution*, a stage model of the revolutionary process based on the experience of the American, French, and Russian revolutions and stressing the reciprocal aspect of the rupture: the crisis of conscience and loss of confidence of the ruling elite above are just as important as the anger and hostility below. Coincidentally, the same year saw the appearance of Roger Bigelow Merriman's *Six Contemporaneous Revolutions*, the work of a historian of the old school and a monument to the doctrine of historical uniqueness. Where Brinton sought and found uniformities, Merriman saw only differences. In part Merriman's results were built into his formulation of the problem: contemporaneous does not equal comparable, and insofar as revolutions are a response to conflicts and tensions common to many societies at similar stages in their development, the appropriate points of comparison will be chronologically dispersed. Also, every historical event *is* unique; but so is every person, which does not prevent us from deriving patterns and uniformities of human behavior.

More recently we have had the two volumes of Robert Palmer on

The Age of the Democratic Revolution, which place the French experience in a larger movement embracing not only the successful revolutions in America and France but also the abortive uprisings in such widely dispersed places as Ireland and Poland. For Palmer, as for Brinton, it takes two to tango: what we have is a general crisis of elites in the face of ideological attacks on the principle of aristocracy, exacerbated in each country by specific local grievances. Even more ambitious in its coverage is the work of Barrington Moore, whose *Social Origins of Dictatorship and Democracy* (1966) examines the pattern of peasant revolts and revolutions in Asia and America as well as Europe, with a view to elucidating the political consequences of modernization. Moore, who feels strongly that statistical analysis has serious limitations, nevertheless believes in the possibility of an objective history based on qualitative data and tries to use comparisons to explain the varied paths of modernization. In the end, he is not ready to offer a model of change: "The allies that peasant discontent can find depends [sic] on the stage of economic development that a country has reached and more specific historical circumstances" (p. 480); and he affirms the element of opportunity in history: in a given situation, things might have gone the other way. The book is a good example of the resistance of history to simplification and of the resistance of the historian to the temptations of simplification.

More focused in its empirical base but equally broad in its implications is the short analysis by William Langer of the revolutions of 1848: again, the emphasis is on the significance of the response from above. Langer argues that where this response was firm and vigorous, as in England, social unrest was never permitted to convert itself into revolution; but where the authorities vacillated, as in Paris, Berlin, and Vienna, the consequence was an escalating recourse to violence.[3]

Finally, mention should be made of an article by James C. Davies, which represents perhaps the only effort since Brinton to produce a model of revolution.[4] Davies, a political scientist, rests his argument on a detailed analysis of three widely different uprisings—

[3] William Langer, "The Pattern of Urban Revolution in 1848," in Evelyn L. Acomb and Marvin L. Brown, Jr., eds., *French Society and Culture since the Old Regime* (New York, 1966), pp. 89–118; also William L. Langer, *Political and Social Upheaval 1832–1852* (New York, 1969).

[4] James C. Davies, "Toward a Theory of Revolution," *American Sociological Review,* XXVII (1962), 5–19.

Dorr's Rebellion (Connecticut, 1842), the Russian Revolution, and the Egyptian Revolution of 1952—and a more rapid examination of the American and French revolutions, the New York draft riots of 1863, and the Nyasaland riots of 1959. His thesis is that "revolutions are likely to occur when a prolonged period of objective economic and social development is followed by a short period of reversal." The operative word is "likely." Since one can think of many instances where such a response has not occurred, this reversal is at best a contributing (necessary?) but not a sufficient condition of revolution.

This is what we might call the Olympian or "macro" approach to the study of revolution: the historian surveys a vast terrain and tries to account for large movements on the national level. Recently, however, in response to a more general interest in social unrest (of which revolutions are only one form), historians have been scrutinizing the revolutionary actor and act in detail in an effort to add a psychological dimension to the conventional analysis of confrontation and conflict. Here too, the French Revolution has furnished matter for inquiry: twenty years ago one would have thought the lemon had been squeezed dry, but the historical school of Albert Soboul and Richard Cobb has shown that there is still a lot of juice left for people who are ready to ask new questions and sit long hours in local archives. These and others, like George Rudé, who has done work on popular movements in England and France, have thrown light on the personality of the revolutionary and on the interaction and reconciliation of revolutionary impulse with the demands of organization and power.[5] Related to this line of inquiry is the work of Eric Hobsbawm, who gave us first, in *Primitive Rebels* (1959), an insight into the character of rebellion in preideological groups and societies—that is, rebellion uninformed by a systematic conception of tactics and strategies or by a mature consideration of ends. Very recently, in *Captain Swing* (1969), Hobsbawm and Rudé have joined to give us a detailed study of one of those improvised, extemporaneous uprisings: the 1830 farm laborers' revolt in England, the last of the "peasant revolts."

[5] See in particular Albert Soboul, *Les sans-culottes parisiens de l'an II* (Paris, 1958); Soboul, *Paysans, Sans-culottes et Jacobins* (Paris, n.d. [1966]); Richard Cobb, *Terreur et subsistances 1793–1795* (Paris, n.d. [1965]); and George Rudé, *The Crowd in the French Revolution* (London, 1959). For a skeptical view of the ideological bias of some of this work, see the essays of Alfred Cobban, *The Social Interpretation of the French Revolution* (Cambridge, 1964), and *Aspects of the French Revolution* (London, 1968).

Methodologically, all this work has been of the classical type, based essentially on the qualitative interpretation of primary sources. The novelty lies in new questions asked, sometimes of new sources, drawn from a variety of contexts to permit comparison. Given the frequency and ubiquity of social conflict, however, the next step was to collect and inspect large numbers of case studies, with a view to deriving by statistical techniques those general characteristics that might otherwise escape attention or be mistaken for the idiosyncrasies of unique events. Historians of nineteenth-century France like Rémi Gossez and Jacques Rougerie, for example, have taken the procedures of Soboul and Rudé one large step further by conducting extensive quantitative analyses of the characteristics of participants in the revolutions of 1848 and the Paris Commune, as revealed in the copious records of deaths, hospital treatment, arrests, and political intelligence left behind by those rebellions. In this way, they have been able to show that lone workers in small shops and traditional crafts, rather than factory workers, remained at the core of urban rebellion; and to establish the relative lack of involvement of the city's many newcomers and its drifters and riffraff—Marx's *Lumpenproletariat*.

Two American projects further illustrate the quantitative approach. One, under the direction of Gilbert Shapiro at the University of Pittsburgh, is sorting by content and source the entire corpus of *cahiers de doléances* (statements of grievances) prepared by French localities, civil bodies, and assemblies of the clergy on the eve of the Revolution of 1789. This is one of the richest and most complete bodies of testimony of social dissatisfaction and aspirations for change extant; generations of historians have already lavished loving and detailed scrutiny on it. Curiously enough, no one has ever before undertaken this kind of overall examination, mainly because of the scope of the task; it is the computer that has made this kind of interpretive census possible (see figure 3-1).

Another project, being carried out by a loose alliance of sociologists and historians in Germany, Canada, and the United States, is inventorying, classifying, and analyzing thousands of uprisings, riots, violent strikes, and the like in France and elsewhere in Europe since around 1800, in an effort to understand the origins, timing, course, and consequences of the different forms of collective violence that arise in modernizing countries.[6] Once again, the raw materials of

[6] See Charles Tilly, "Collective Violence in European Perspective," in Hugh Davis Graham and Ted Robert Gurr, eds., *Violence in America* (Washington: U. S. Government Printing Office, 1969), pp. 4–45.

the inquiry—police reports, newspaper accounts, censuses, surveys of industry, and so on—are relatively familiar to historians. What is different is the scale of the enterprise, the insistence on quantification and computerization of a substantial part of the materials, and, most important, the way of asking the questions.

The originators of these two projects are sociologists by training. But some young historians have found their procedure interesting and valuable enough to join forces with them. As a result, still another generation of scholars is coming along, combining both the conventional qualitative and the newer quantitative methods, and examining those aspects of social unrest which seem especially important in the light of our own experience: the timing of conflict, the determinants of violence, the nature of the response by the authorities, the psychological and social frontier between rebels and forces of order, the choice and imposition of sanctions, the process of appeasement, and the choice between prevention and cure.

Revolution as a form of social unrest is only one focal theme among many. One could do a similar capsule history of research on such subjects as war, or power, or poverty, or contacts between races and civilizations. In each case changing experience and concerns have generated new lines of inquiry, which have been enriched by and have enriched in turn parallel research in other disciplines. In the area of imperialism and colonialism, for example, the traditional concentration on the high-level maneuvers and arrangements of distant diplomats and officials in London, Paris, and Madrid has long since given way to an interest in the meaning of the imperial relationship for the populations concerned, both dominant and subordinate; and the quality of this aspect of the inquiry has been enormously enhanced, first, by the use of new sources on the everyday character of colonial domination (including the records and testimony of the subject peoples themselves), and second, by concepts and insights derived from psychology and even psychiatry. This transfer from other disciplines of insights often derived from the study of different subjects in different times and places entails obvious hazards; and the historian who leaps from psychoanalysis in revolutionary Algeria to the interpretation of the Chinese response to European pressure a hundred years earlier, or from Nazi concentration camps to American plantation slavery does so at some peril to his scholarly soul. Yet this is just the kind of risk that the conscientious historian, thanks to his canons of evidence, is well equipped to take. This is not to say that these conceptual imports will make possible a history any more definitive than what has gone before. They open up new kinds and levels of understanding, and there will be other kinds and levels to follow. This endless process of explora-

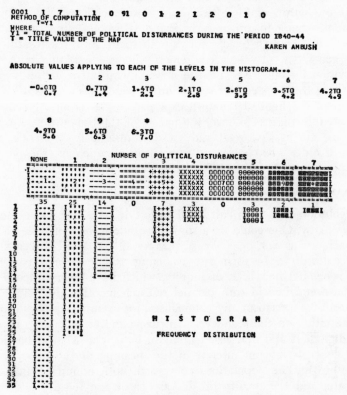

FIGURE 3-1   COMPUTER-PREPARED MAP OF VIOLENT INCI-
DENTS IN FRANCE, 1840–1844

Research by Charles Tilly.

tion and discovery is intellectually one of the most exciting features of the discipline: there is always room for a new idea or a fresh approach.

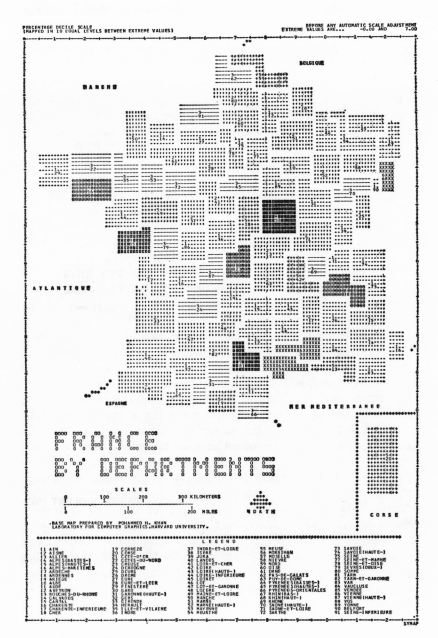

BELGIQUE

MANCHE

ATLANTIQUE

ESPAGNE

MER MEDITERRANEE

CORSE

SCALES

0   100   200   300 KILOMETERS

0   100   200 MILES   NORTH

BASE MAP PREPARED BY MOHAMMED H. KHAN
LABORATORY FOR COMPUTER GRAPHICS, HARVARD UNIVERSITY.

LEGEND

1 AIN	19 CORREZE	37 INDRE-ET-LOIRE	55 MEUSE	73 SAVOIE
2 AISNE	20 CORSE	38 ISERE	56 MORBIHAN	74 SAVOIE(HAUTE-)
3 ALLIER	21 COTES-D'CR	39 JURA	57 MOSELLE	75 SEINE
4 ALPES(BASSES-)	22 COTES-DU-NORD	40 LANDES	58 NIEVRE	76 SEINE-ET-MARNE
5 ALPES(HAUTE-)	23 CREUSE	41 LOIR-ET-CHER	59 NORD	77 SEINE-ET-OISE
6 ALPES-MARITIMES	24 DORDOGNE	42 LOIRE	60 OISE	78 SEVRES(DEUX-)
7 ARDECHE	25 DOURS	43 LOIRE(HAUTE-)	61 ORNE	80 SOMME
8 ARDENNES	26 DROME	44 LOIRE-INFERIEURE	62 PAS-DE-CALAIS	81 TARN
9 ARIEGE	27 EURE	45 LOIRET	63 PUY-DE-DOME	82 TARN-ET-GARONNE
10 AUBE	28 EURE-ET-LOIR	46 LOT	64 PYRENEES(BASSES-)	83 VAR
11 AUDE	29 FINISTERE	47 LOT-ET-GARONNE	65 PYRENEES(HAUTES-)	84 VAUCLUSE
12 AVEYRON	30 GARD	48 LOZERE	66 PYRENEES-ORIENTALES	85 VENDEE
13 BOUCHE-DU-RHONE	31 GARONNE(HAUTE-)	49 MAINE-ET-LOIRE	67 RHIN(BAS-)	86 VIENNE
14 CALVADOS	32 GERS	50 MANCHE	68 RHIN(HAUT-)	87 VIENNE(HAUTE-)
15 CANTAL	33 GIRONDE	51 MARNE	69 RHONE	88 VOS
16 CHARENTE	34 HERAULT	52 MARNE(HAUTE-)	70 SAONE(HAUTE-)	89 YONNE
17 CHARENTE-INFERIEURE	35 ILLE-ET-VILAINE	53 MAYENNE	71 SAONE-ET-LOIRE	90 BELFORT
18 CHER	36 INDRE	54 MEURTHE	72 SARTHE	91 SEINE-INFERIEURE

SYMAP

47

PREMODERN HISTORY

Nothing illustrates the endless possibilities for reinterpretation better than the effects of innovation in so long-established and minutely scrutinized a field as ancient history. This has always been looked on as a kind of compact enclosure, within which the corpus of evidence was limited, known, and accessible almost in its entirety to any individual researcher who chose to make the effort. One would have thought the opportunities for new departures and major revisions were correspondingly limited, as generations of scholars seemingly plowed and replowed the same ground.

Yet in the last generation, a number of major contributions have appeared, based on the application of new techniques borrowed from other fields of history and other disciplines and improved in the process of adaptation. One of the most interesting methodologically is Ronald Syme's use of prosopography to analyze the composition, connections, and comportment of the Roman ruling classes during the transition from Republic to Empire. This technique of collective biography had already been used with great success by Lewis Namier in his study of the British governing elite in the eighteenth century, but it was potentially even more important in ancient history, where numerical data are almost entirely wanting, but where the availability of abundant but scattered biographical material make it possible to move from the individual and idiosyncratic to the general and representative. By investigating the links between various clans, the role of personal obligations and patronage, and the character of family feuds, Syme and other practitioners of this approach have revealed a whole new dimension of Roman politics previously obscured by the nineteenth-century obsession with "parties" and the reduction of Roman politics to a struggle between the "oligarchs" and the "democrats." [7]

This new interpretation has not gone unchallenged. The sharpest attack has come from Christian Meier, in his *Res Publica Amissa* (1966), who has been especially skeptical of the too easy comparison of Republican Rome and eighteenth-century Britain. In Rome, he notes, the Senate was the government; in England, the Parliament

[7] See among others Ronald Syme, *The Roman Revolution* (1938); L. R. Taylor, *Party Politics in the Age of Caesar* (1949); E. Badian, *Foreign Clientelae* (1958).

was set over against the government. In Rome, men were divided by major political issues; in England, by competition for spoils and office. For Meier, the Roman elite was essentially united in important matters, whereas shifts in alignments over petty matters of personal dignity were so frequent that it is impossible to speak of a system of factions.

Much of this criticism is well taken; but some of it incorrectly assumes that the influence of personal and family connections excludes the presence of other factors and that one can invalidate the prosopographical approach by showing that it will not explain everything. Most scholars, moreover, are inclined to distinguish between good and bad historiography and between one period of Roman history and another. The debate is still open and even the older emphasis on class conflict is far from dead: drawing some of his inspiration from Rudé's work on the French mob of the eighteenth century, P. A. Brunt finds the main cause of the fall of the Roman Republic in agrarian discontents.[8] This counterpoint of consideration and reconsideration is, as we have seen, at the heart of the process of the advancement of historical knowledge.

At the same time, the boundaries of the corpus of evidence on the premodern period have been pushed back by new scientific techniques borrowed from the natural sciences: the use of aerial photography to locate remains invisible on the ground; the measurement of carbon-14 traces as a way of dating archaeological objects; the application of glotto-chronology to establish time-depth in languages; the use of botanical knowledge and methods to study the diet, numbers, migrations, and patterns of settlement of earlier peoples; the application of historical geology and geography to examine the record of climatic change, with all its consequences for food supply and the life, death, and movement of populations; the use of spectrography and chemical analysis to verify the authenticity and origin of artifacts and establish the techniques that went into their manufacture. We have also seen, in Ventris's spectacular decipherment of Linear B (see fig. 3-2), the highly successful application of cryptanalytic and linguistic (as against philological) techniques to the understanding of unknown tongues. (The variety and ingenuity of this collaboration between history and archaeology on the one hand and the natural sciences on the other convey as nothing else the breadth and open-endedness of what is meant by interdisciplinary

[8] P. A. Brunt, "The Roman Mob," *Past and Present*, XXXV (December, 1966), 1–27.

LINEAR SCRIPT B SYLLABIC GRID
(2ND STATE)

DIAGNOSIS OF CONSONANT AND VOWEL EQUATIONS   ATHENS, 28 SEPT 51
IN THE INFLEXIONAL MATERIAL FROM PYLOS:

Left-margin (vertical) note: THESE 51 SIGNS MAKE UP 90% OF ALL SIGN OCCURRENCES IN THE PYLOS SIGNGROUP INDEX. APPENDED FIGURES GIVE EACH SIGN'S OVERALL FREQUENCY PER MILLE IN THE PYLOS INDEX.

Column-group headings:

"Impure" ending, typical syllables before -ỉ & -Ə in Case 2c & 3	"Pure" ending, typical nominatives of forms in Column I	Includes possible "accusatives"	Also, but less frequently, the nominatives of forms in Column I
THESE SIGNS DON'T OCCUR BEFORE -[sign]-	THESE SIGNS OCCUR LESS COMMONLY OR NOT AT ALL BEFORE -[sign]-		
MORE OFTEN FEMININE THAN MASCULINE?	"MORE OFTEN MASCULINE THAN FEMININE?		MORE OFTEN FEMININE THAN MASCULINE?
NORMALLY FORM THE GENITIVE SINGULAR BY ADDING -ỉ	NORMALLY FORM THE GENITIVE SINGULAR BY ADDING -[sign]		

consonant	vowel 1	vowel 2	vowel 3	vowel 4	vowel 5
pure vowels?	[sign] 30.3				[sign] 37.2
a semi-vowel?			[sign] 34.0	[sign] 29.4	
1	[sign] 14.8	[sign] 32.5	[sign] 21.2	[sign]³ 28.1	[sign] 18.8
2	[sign] 19.6	[sign] 17.5			[sign] 13.7
3		[sign] 9.2		[sign] 3.3	[sign] 10.0
4	[sign] 17.0	[sign] 28.6			[sign] 0.4
5	[sign] 17.7	[sign] 10.3		[sign] 4.1	[sign] 10.2
6	[sign] 7.4	[sign] 20.5		[sign] 14.8	[sign] 14.4
7	[sign] 4.1	[sign] 44.0			
8	[sign] 6.1	[sign] 6.1		[sign] 13.5	[sign] 15.2
9		[sign] 33.1		[sign] 32.3	[sign] 2.4
10	[sign] 22.2		[sign] 38.2	[sign] 3.5	[sign] 2.2
11	[sign] 31.2	[sign] 33.8	[sign] 34.4	[sign] 8.3	[sign] 0.7
12	[sign] 17.0			[sign] 37.7	[sign] 24.0
13		[sign] 9.4	[sign] 14.2		
14	[sign] 5.0				
15	[sign] 12.6				

MICHAEL VENTRIS

FIGURE 3-2   MICHAEL VENTRIS' GRID FOR DECODING OF LINEAR B

From John Chadwick, *The Decipherment of Linear B*, 2nd ed. (Cambridge: Cambridge University Press, 1968), p. 59. Reprinted by permission of the publisher.

history. Our primary concern in this report is with the links between history and the social and behavioral sciences, but these are only part of a much larger set of alliances.)

Even the lack of numerical information may some day yield to the persistent effort to quantify whenever possible. Students of the premodern world have begun to work through graveyards in an effort to learn something about age at death, life expectancy, and possible population change. David Herlihy has built some bold hypotheses on the fluctuating volume of land transactions in medieval Italy. Others have been scrutinizing Athenian tribute lists as a clue to the foreign relations and economic currents of the period. The time may yet come when someone attempts a kind of aggregate income series for certain parts and periods of the premodern world. Economic theorists insist that something can be done, while classical and medieval scholars warn against this kind of "creative" history. Still, the work of the so-called "New Economic History" and the techniques of family reconstitution developed in historical demography are evidence that more can be done than we would yesterday have thought possible.

ECONOMIC HISTORY

The branch of history best suited to the quantitative techniques usually associated with science or social science is probably economic history. For one thing, the subject matter of economic history—the output of goods and services, employment, incomes, prices, and the like—is susceptible of measurement; what is more, the units of measurement can usually (though not always) be standardized sufficiently to permit comparisons in space and time. For another, economic history has the advantage of dealing with a domain that has been the object of considerable abstract analysis. It can draw on, test, and be guided by the highly developed corpus of economic theory, by comparison with which the theoretical foundations of other branches of history are thin and spotty. This is not to say that economic theory is a kind of infallible dogma; the persistence of disagreement among economists is evidence enough of the absence of an immutable orthodoxy. Even so, theory provides the economic historian with a conceptual framework and patterns of relationship that serve as both stimulus and control to his research.

Not all economic history is informed by the concerns or conceptions of economic theory. Quite the contrary: most economic historians have never received sufficient training in economics to marry the two disciplines successfully; and this gap has clearly widened as economics has become increasingly mathematical and hence unreadable to many historians. But a small and flourishing group of younger scholars, the so-called cliometricians, have in recent years come to economic history from economics, and these have done much to enhance the theoretical and quantitative character of the field. They are the exponents of the New Economic History, which they distinguish from the old

1. by its recourse to explicit explanatory models, relevant to if not necessarily consonant with economic theory and expressed if possible in mathematical terms; 2. by the verification of these models with quantitative data; 3. by the measurement of phenomena previously deemed unmeasurable, sometimes by the invention of surrogate variables that connote indirectly the object of investigation; 4. by acceptance of and attention to relations of cause and effect and the utilization in this regard of contrafactual hypotheses: to say that A is the cause of B implies that if no A, then no B. What, Robert Fogel has asked, if there had been no railroad? What would the American economy have been like? [9] This is the kind of question that historians have usually tried to avoid, on the principle that history is not concerned with might-have-beens. What if there had been no Napoleon? But there was a Napoleon. The merit of the New Economic History is to have shown that insofar as scholars have assigned a historical role to Napoleon, they have in fact been saying something about what might have been.

The New Economic History, like most such innovations, is not so new as its partisans would have one believe. One must go back at least as far as the essays of Walt W. Rostow on the British economy in the nineteenth century (published in 1948, but including articles that had appeared much earlier) for the first serious and successful effort by an economic historian to analyze history with the aid of economic theory while testing economic theory by the data of history.[10] But the recent surge of work in this field goes back about a

[9] Robert W. Fogel, *Railroads and American Economic Growth: Essays in Econometric History* (Baltimore, 1964).
[10] W. W. Rostow, *British Economy of the Nineteenth Century* (Oxford, 1949).

decade—to the essays of Alfred Conrad and John Meyer on the character of slavery in the antebellum South.[11] The question that Conrad and Meyer addressed themselves to was one that had been long and fiercely debated by historians: Did slavery pay? The question seems innocent enough, but it is loaded politically: for if slavery did not pay and hence was doomed, then one could argue, as some Southern sympathizers did, that the war was not necessary; or worse yet for Northern supporters, that the war was provoked and fought for crass political and material reasons. Conrad and Meyer showed, by a comparison of the cost of rearing and holding slaves with their market value, that slavery did pay, even in the Old South, which could no longer compete in agriculture with cheaper lands to the West: if you couldn't use slaves profitably on a plantation, you could still breed them profitably for those who could use them. Conrad and Meyer did not discover anything; they simply confirmed in a new and especially convincing way a position that other historians, using more conventional qualitative data, had already advanced. Yet confirmation is an important gain in so highly controversial an area.

Since Conrad and Meyer were proving something already known if not universally accepted, their findings stirred up interest, but not a storm. It has been quite otherwise with the work of Robert Fogel, who began his research as a believer in the primacy of the railroad in the creation of a unified industrial economy in the United States, but who after research concluded that the contribution of the iron horse was far smaller than conventionally assumed. In principle, Fogel wanted to test the proposition that the railroad was indispensable to American development (he actually found one or two scholars who had said as much). Such a proposition is either a truism —in the sense that anything today has some influence on tomorrow and hence is indispensable to it—or a form of hyperbole, in which case it is easily disprovable, for to every technique there is an alternative (if only the technique it has displaced). In fact, what Fogel was really testing was the importance of the railway, and to this end he did take the earlier techniques of canal and wagon transport and asked what the United States would have been like if it had had to continue to rely on these for the movement of persons and goods. This, of course, is where contrafactual history gets hazardous: it is one thing to ask this kind of question and treat it in the abstract;

[11] Alfred H. Conrad and John R. Meyer, "The Economics of Slavery in the Ante Bellum South," *Journal of Political Economy*, LXVI (April, 1958), reprinted in Conrad and Meyer, *The Economics of Slavery* (Chicago, 1964), pp. 43–114.

it is quite another to imagine what might have happened and build
a sequence of eventuality on hypothetical data.

It would be impossible here to follow Fogel's extremely ingenious
calculations in detail. Suffice it to say that on the basis of the studies
of army engineers, he concluded that in the absence of the railway,
a canal and river system could (would) have been built that could
have served almost all the agricultural and mineral land east of the
Rockies at a cost only slightly higher than that of the rail network
that was actually constructed. The nation that resulted would have
been significantly different because of the relative isolation of the
Pacific states. But national income, he reckons, would have been only
a few percentage points lower in 1890 than it actually was: perhaps
3 or 4 percent on the basis of one set of assumptions, as high as 6
or 7 percent on others.

This inevitably raises the question, how important is 3 percent
or 7 percent? And this is not the kind of question that is easy to
answer, since so much depends on how one defines importance.[12]
In the meantime, Fogel has clearly shown that the contribution of
the railroad to the American economy was less than had usually
been assumed; and this demonstration was so upsetting to those
brought up on conventional doctrine (including railway historians,
who are a sentimental breed) that it has stirred up a fierce controversy.[13] This in turn has been all to the good, for it has stimulated
further research in this area, as well as on other subjects to which
these techniques are applicable.

In the last decade, the output of econometric history has increased
spectacularly, especially in the United States. One of the most effective promoters of this development has been the Purdue Seminar

[12] A similar question is posed by the work of Peter McClelland, who calculates
the loss to the American colonists due to British interference in overseas trade
in the period before the Revolution at 3 percent of gross product. The implication is that the economic issue was not important enough to be a major cause
of the Revolution. But can we make that inference? Or was this kind of loss,
the result of a system in which the colonists had no direct representation in
Parliament and felt themselves at the mercy of whatever vested interests in
Britain could gain the ear of the government, cause for vexation and an incite-
ment to violence? See McClelland's address to a session of the 1968 meeting of
the American Economic Association, "The Cost to America of British Imperial
Policy," *American Economic Review*, LIX (May, 1969), 370–82, and Jonathon
R. T. Hughes's comments, ibid., pp. 382–85.
[13] For the latest contribution to the controversy, along with footnote references
to most of the earlier literature, see Paul A. David, "Transportation Innovation
and Economic Growth: Professor Fogel on and off the Rails," *Economic History
Review*, 2nd ser., XXII (1969), 506–25.

on Quantitative Methods in Economic History, which has convened annually since December, 1960, and brought together dozens of the "bright young men" in this area and helped turn a few isolated articles into a field of inquiry. It would be impossible to review all the important contributions, but a brief list will illustrate the variety and range of this research: John Meyer has used input-output analysis to weigh the effect of changes in the volume of British trade on the rate of British economic growth in the late nineteenth century; William Whitney has used similar techniques to measure the effect of tariffs on the rise of manufacturing in the United States after the Civil War; Peter Temin has challenged the traditional view that the diffusion of the Bessemer process was the key to the rapid development of the American steel industry; Douglass North, in a study of productivity gains in oceanic shipping, and Robert Zevin, in an analysis of the growth of the American textile industry, have depreciated the contribution of technological advance relative to such factors as increasing scale, efficiencies of organization and management, and improving quality of labor. And H. J. Habakkuk, Temin, Fogel, and Nathan Rosenberg, in an exchange that still continues, have done much to clarify the much debated question of the determinants of the relative proportions of labor and capital in industrial production in the United States and Great Britain in the nineteenth century.

The success of the New Economic History, which is to be measured as much in its recruitment of new talent as in its work, has led Robert Fogel, its most ardent spokesman, to call for the diffusion of similar mathematical and statistical techniques to other branches of history. To this end, the Mathematical Social Science Board has created a Committee on Mathematical and Statistical Methods in History, which has begun by surveying the literature (small but growing faster all the time), calling meetings of interested parties as a device to stimulate work, and encouraging the production of teaching materials to facilitate the training of mathematically competent historians. The committee recognize that "general history," as they call it, is less susceptible of statistical and mathematical treatment than economic history; also that other kinds of historians will be less receptive to or attracted by these techniques than economic historians. (One should note in this connection that the increasingly mathematical character of economic history has had the initial consequence of driving historians away from the field. Those who might have once worked in this area are now more likely to turn to social history.) Even so, the committee feel that insofar as these techniques work, that is, increase the historian's power to understand his subject, they will find practitioners.

In the meantime, what of the potential contribution of econometric history? It is still too early to say. There will always be subjects not amenable to quantitative analysis, and on the strength of such cliometric work as has been done, it seems fair to say that some of the most important and interesting problems in economic history fall into this recalcitrant category. In general, the bigger the subject and the greater its ramifications, the harder to reduce it to a model susceptible of statistical verification. The new economic history seems to work best on carefully delimited issues.

Still we should not underestimate the possibilities of an ingenious quantitative approach, both in creating new data and finding new ways to deal with incomplete data. Moreover, the path of advance in other disciplines has also been characterized by this conscious delimitation and focusing of research to suit the means and knowledge of the researcher. It may be that what starts here as a narrowing will eventually broaden our possibilities considerably.

DEMOGRAPHIC HISTORY

Population studies bring historians close to matters of public policy. For centuries governments and their critics have based important programs for public welfare, economic development, and defense on assumptions about the long-run trend in population growth and it determinants. Strange as it seems today, many prominent eighteenth-century thinkers believed the population of Western countries had been declining for a long time as part of a general decay of society. When Malthus began to argue, toward the end of the century, that population not only was growing but also had a natural tendency to grow faster than resources, he simultaneously challenged widespread historical opinion and suggested that most proposals for agricultural improvement and poor relief were self-defeating. The connection with policy remains today. Many scholars hope that an understanding of how the birth rate actually went down in Western countries over the last few centuries will help the many countries now burdened with swelling populations to check their rate of growth.

Over the past twenty years, historical studies of population have produced some of the most fruitful exchanges between history and the other social sciences. Historical demography is not a new field; demographers themselves often date the founding of their discipline by the publication in 1662 of John Graunt's *Natural and Political Observations Made Upon the Bills of Mortality*, a work dealing with English population data extending back into the sixteenth century. But historical demography is a renewed field, because since 1940 students of population have developed powerful ideas and procedures for connecting analysis of the present with analyses of the past.

Before that time, demographers considering both the Western experience and the contemporary populations of the rest of the world had developed a theory of demographic transition which they hoped would forecast the impact of industrialization on population throughout the world. Roger Revelle recently summed it up:

> In the past, according to this theory, human populations maintained themselves or slowly expanded under conditions of high mortality balanced against high, essentially uncontrolled fertility. During the Industrial Revolution, fertility remained high and uncontrolled for a while, and the average length of life increased. As a result, populations grew rapidly in the Western world, at rates higher than ever before experienced. During the nineteenth and early twentieth centuries, birth rates began to come down, first in France and the United States, due to the deliberate control of births by individual couples. This decline in fertility eventually slowed down population growth. . . .[14]

The theory has practical implications, since it suggests that improving public health without industrialization will produce extremely fast population growth, whereas industrialization will more or less automatically stabilize the population.

At first, many historical demographers took the general validity of demographic transition theory for granted and tried mainly to discover how and when the transition occurred in various Western countries. Then the widespread and unexpected rise in fertility in Western countries after 1940, the stubbornness of population problems outside the West, and the accumulating findings of historical

[14] Roger Revelle, "Introduction" to the issue "Historical Population Studies," *Daedalus* (Spring, 1968), p. 353.

research itself all turned them toward a reexamination of the entire process, beginning with the pretransitional stage.

Going back this far posed a difficult problem. Regular and reasonably complete census data for the countries of Western Europe go back only to the beginning of the nineteenth century; for the United States, to 1790. The only major exception is Sweden, with censuses from the middle of the eighteenth century. In order to study, therefore, the early stages of the demographic transition, a way had to be found to "reconstitute" the population record from such incomplete and irregular data as have come down to us.

The technical breakthrough came in France. There, a group of demographers and historians around Louis Henry developed a method for detecting changes in patterns of birth, death, and marriage for periods before the existence of modern censuses and vital statistics. This method of *family reconstitution* consists of reconstructing the demographic histories of individual families, event by event, from genealogies, parish registers of baptisms, or similar records, and then aggregating the data in various ways to arrive at estimates of vital rates for an entire community. Since the French first devised the procedure, it has been widely used in France, England, the rest of Europe, and the United States.

Family reconstitution and other new ways of doing historical demography have changed our understanding of European life before the nineteenth century. Some of the most important findings are those of the Cambridge (England) Group for the History of Population and Social Structure, under the direction of Peter Laslett and E. A. Wrigley (see fig. 3-3). The preliminary returns of what is planned to be a representative sample of British communities in the seventeenth and eighteenth centuries show, for example, that the typical household was small, composed of the nuclear family and, often, servants; and that geographical mobility was higher than anyone has suspected. In effect, the British population of this period was in frequent motion—something like a Brownian movement—much more so than populations on the Continent. If these findings are confirmed by further research, they would have obvious importance for an understanding of the precocity of Britain's economic and technological development: a mobile population implies a more efficient labor market and a more rapid diffusion of techniques.

The new methods for the study of population history have also made possible important revisions in the theory of the demographic transition. Two findings in particular have made a difference to historical thinking. The first is the variability and rationality of demographic behavior. The conventional assumption had been Malthusian: that preindustrial populations were more or less uniformly characterized by high, relatively stable fertility and high, unstable mortality, with women marrying young and bearing children incessantly. Yet we now know that European and American women of the preindustrial era married rather late and did not bear anything like the number of children they could have. What is more, historians have discovered substantial variations from time to time and place to place, not only in fertility, but in such matters as age at marriage, life expectancy, premarital intercourse, and legitimacy rates. A survey by Robert Wells of Quaker families in pre- and post-colonial America, for example, shows a decline in the average size of the completed family from 6.7 to 5.0 children—a large drop; and a study by James Somerville of families in Salem, Massachusetts, shows the mean age at marriage for females rising from 20.8 years in the seventeenth century to 22.4 years in the eighteenth.[15]

Similarly, the pattern of population change in eighteenth-century France was markedly different from that of other European countries in the same period. The evidence is not all in, but everything we know points not only to the wide practice of birth control (which was not peculiar to France), but to birth control so employed as to produce, beginning in the last quarter of the century, a fall in the birth rate. This was unique, for birth rates elsewhere were rising, if anything, in these years and were to remain at a high level more suited to pretransitional mortality rates long after the death rate had turned downward. Because of the precocity of this adaptation, France, which in the seventeenth and eighteenth centuries was far and away the most populous and powerful nation in Europe, never really shared in the population explosion of the industrial period and lost forever the political preeminence she had enjoyed under Louis XIV and Napoleon.

The second major contribution of these researches is to emphasize the distinctiveness of the European experience. Few populations anywhere in the world satisfy the Malthusian model of maximum fertility corrected at intervals by "dismal peaks" of mortality. On the whole, however, Europe stands out from the rest of the world by its successful reliance on preconceptional arrangements for the limita-

[15] See the report of the "Stony Brook Conference on Social History," October 24–25, 1969, in *Historical Methods Newsletter* (University of Pittsburgh), III, no. 1 (December, 1969), 12–13.

MARRIAGE

M | 237 | place COLYTON | date 21-1-1570 | date of end 27-4-1601 | date of next 31-8-1601

LITERACY

L | / | husband / | wife /

HUSBAND

H | surname HORE | name(s) WILLIAM | date of baptism(birth) 3-1-1544 | date of burial(death) 16-4-1611

residence (occupation) at marriage -- COLYTON (SHOEMAKER) | residence (occupation) at burial COLYTON | date 15801 - (SHOEMAKER) | residence (occupation)

order of marr. ≥1 | earlier FRF no. | later FRF no. 599 | residence at baptism COLYTON

Husband's father

HF | surname = | name(s) HARRY | residence (occupation) COLYTON | FRF no. 152

Husband's mother

HM | surname CONNANTE | name(s) AGNES

WIFE

W | surname BYRDE | name(s) JOHANE | date of baptism(birth) 7-1-1548 | date of burial(death) 27-4-1601

residence (occupation) at marriage -- COLYTON | residence (occupation) at burial COLYTON | date | residence (occupation)

order of marr. | earlier FRF no. | later FRF no. | residence at baptism COLYTON

Wife's father

WF | surname = | name(s) JOHN | FRF no.

Wife's mother

WM | surname | name(s)

CHILDREN

	sex	date of baptism(birth)	date of burial(death)	status	name(s)	date of marriage	FRF no. of first marr.	surname of spouse	age at bur.	age at marr.	birth interval	age of mother
1 C	F	24-7-1570			KATREN						6	22
2 C	F	27-1-1572			ANNE						18	24
3 C	F	22-5-1575	16-5-1627	W	AGNES	7-3-1603	620	SCARSE	51	27	39	27
4 C	M	28-2-1577		S	RYCHARD						21	29
5 C	M	17-4-1579	14-5-1579	S	HENRY				28d		25	31
6 C	F	2-3-1580			ELSABETHE						10	32

7	C	F	27-5-1582	31-8-1602	1s	CHARITYE			/
8	C	F	16-10-1584	27-10-1584	1s	SYTHE			/
9	C	F	24-4-1586	2-3-1663	1s	EDDYTHE			/
10	C	M	15-12-1588			HENRY			/
11	C	M	28-9-1591	2-12-1658	W	EDWARD	5-6-1615	8.17	SALTER	/
12	C									/
13	C									/
14	C									/
15	C									/
16	C									/

FRF iv 67

	Age group	Years marr.	No.of births
	15 - 19		
	20 - 24	20	24 34	2
	25 - 29	110	28 36	2
	30 - 34	76	18 38	3
	35 - 39		31 40	2
	40 - 44	67 23	33 43	2
	45 - 49			0

	Husband	Wife
Age at marriage	26	22
Age at end of marriage	57	53
Age at burial	67	
Length of widowhood (mths)	4	
Length of marriage (years)	31	
	total	sons	daughters
	11	4	7
Number of births	11	

COMMENTS

FIGURE 3-3 FAMILY RECONSTITUTION FORM, USED IN HISTORICAL DEMOGRAPHY

From research directed by E. A. Wrigley. Reproduced by permission of Professor Wrigley. Information below and to the right of the double line would not ordinarily be written in by hand, but would be derived by computer from the information on the rest of the form.

61

tion of population: late marriage, selective permanent celibacy, and birth control. The only major population that gives evidence of a similar pattern is that of Tokugawa Japan. This is no small matter, for there is no better sign of a commitment to rational, controlled behavior than its application in this most intimate area of life. The implications of these inquiries, therefore, far transcend the realm of population proper; by shedding light on one of the deepest values of European society (and its non-European offshoots), the demographer has added a new element to the dossier of the history of rationality and rationalization, which embraces such diverse phenomena as the development of bureaucratic administration, the advance of science and technology, and the rise of new forms of commercial and industrial organization.

All of this is interesting history. It may turn out to be even more important as a contribution to our understanding of contemporary population processes. The net effect of this work in historical demography is to loosen the close connection once thought to exist between the demographic transition and industrialization. The new findings give more importance to rural conditions: the interdependence of marriage and inheritance of land, the effects of community controls over marriage and child-bearing, and the fluctuations of the agrarian economy. Contraceptive techniques show up in history, not as innovations, but as something that in one form or another was already there, before the demographic transition began. The question of preconceptional birth control then becomes one of learning why a given population made use of these techniques. This transformation of the problem, in turn, has obvious implications for today's antinatalist campaigns, which have laid heavy stress on the diffusion of new and more potent anticonceptional devices. There is nothing so congenial as to have recourse to what is sometimes called a "technological fix"—a new piece of hardware or a new way of doing things that solves a complex difficulty. Yet the demographers and social engineers who have mounted these campaigns have found that it is one thing to have the fix and another to persuade people to use it. They would do well to study population history.

THE AREA APPROACH

We have already remarked on the impetus given by so-called area research centers to interdisciplinary work. They have brought together scholars from different fields to work side by side, and proximity has promoted communication, with favorable effects on both the quality of research and the attractiveness of these fields to young historians. Unfortunately, these centers have been concerned almost exclusively with what are sometimes called the exotic areas of the globe: East Asia, Latin America, Africa, tropical regions, the Middle East, and Soviet Russia. American and European studies have benefited little from this approach, in large part because they are better known and have always received their full share of attention (from indigenous as well as American scholars in the case of European countries); the foundations that have funded most of the area programs have aimed precisely at strengthening expertise where it was weakest. The medicine has worked well, so well that it is now apparent that the older fields of history could well use a similar "shot in the arm" to wrench them out of conventional paths and stimulate them to more cross-disciplinary work.

Of the "exotic" areas, East Asia has perhaps the longest and most illustrious historiographical tradition; the only competitor for the honor would be Russian history. The field has always drawn talented and dedicated researchers, if only because the language skills required act as a screen to keep out the weak and faint-hearted. Since World War II, East Asian history has enjoyed something of a flowering, partly because of the influx of language specialists trained during the war by the armed forces, partly because the much enhanced American interest in the area justified and encouraged generous funding. One result has been an active exploration of the comparative and interdisciplinary aspects of history.

Historians writing of Asia in Western languages have always been casually comparative, but in recent years their comparisons have become increasingly explicit and well informed. The experience of the West is always present and relevant. Thus nearly all economic histories of China and Japan refer to contrasts in timing, leadership, speed, and patterns of growth with one or another Western country. Much of this is subtle and thoughtful, and the almost compulsory adoption of a comparative stance has served to focus attention on topics and problems that might otherwise have been neglected.

At the same time, the influence of area study programs has been to foster an interdisciplinary approach to research, with special emphasis on the marriage of history with the other social sciences. Among other things, control of research funds has usually been in the hands of interdisciplinary committees, and scholarship here as elsewhere has been responsive to money. As a result, the historian of China, Japan, or India has been more attentive to the work of anthropologists, linguists, sociologists, and lawyers than his colleague in medieval English or colonial American history.

Ronald Dore's book on *City Life in Japan* is an excellent example. Dore, trained in the Japanese language in a military program during World War II, went on afterward to study Japanese literature and then from that to become a sociologist and historian. His book applies both disciplines to the examination of a Tokyo ward in the early 1950s, with long and penetrating flashbacks into earlier periods. The book begins like a novel: We walk the streets of the ward, hear the sounds, watch the movement, meet the resident families. Then we hear about housing, getting and spending, health and security, conjugal relations, neighborliness and friendship, education, leisure, and religion. Each subject is placed in a historical perspective two or three generations deep. Sometimes Mr. Dore goes even further back: his discussion of the family in the Tokugawa period (1603–1867) is the only extended treatment of the subject in a Western language.

Frederick Wakeman's *Strangers at the Gate: Social Disorder in South China, 1839–1861* combines history with anthropology to illuminate the course of political change. It is a study of the effects of the Opium War (1839–42) on Chinese society in the Yangtze delta. These are examined on two levels. First, there was the general response to the foreign incursion. Wakeman argues that the Opium War caused ethnic stereotypes to become racist xenophobia. Previously the Cantonese had formed *relatively* tolerant, condescending notions of Western behavior. Foreigners had been represented as uncouth barbarians, unworthy of serious attention. Under the stress of violence and defeat, this image was drastically transformed. The foreigner was now a depraved monster threatening the virtue of Chinese women. Some historians have insisted that this xenophobia was the first version of Chinese nationalism. Wakeman feels that such a view is anachronistic and reads later developments too far into the past. The fear and hatred were still too local and as a consequence they engendered urban patriotism, not nationalism. Still, it was a beginning, and it was this milieu that produced one of the fathers of modern Chinese nationalism, Sun Yat-sen.

Secondly, the book analyzes the forms of rural disorder that came in the wake of war. Even before the war there had been a proliferation of secret societies of lawbreakers; now they profited from the confusion and breakdown of authority to increase their depredations. The consequent insecurity led some to turn to religious consolations, and one sectarian group, the millenarian Society of God Worshippers, rose up against the imperial regime. The fighting that followed was bitter as only civil war aggravated by religious passions can be: before the Taiping Rebellion was put down, some twenty million people were killed.

All of this had a devastating effect on the structure of kinship and society. Whereas Chinese rulers had always made it a point to keep local notables from usurping the authority of the central government, even forbidding officials to serve in their home provinces, now, in this time of troubles, local gentry were able to form private militias and tyrannize over the population. Whereas the traditional clans had united rich and poor members of the same lineage and mitigated class conflict, the new militias enabled the notables to dominate the clans and drain their income into their own pockets. Poorer kinsmen grew disaffected, swelled the ranks of secret societies and private militias, and thereby strengthened the forces of violence and selfishness. More and more the gentry became identified as social parasites. Warlordism and rural revolution were spawned together.

Neither the Dore nor the Wakeman book is a patent example of social-scientific history. Neither is quantitative; neither is conscientiously explicit about its methodology. The Dore book, to be sure, for all its historical dimension, is an exercise in contemporary urban sociology; but the Wakeman study is essentially a highly enriched piece of traditional historiography. In this sense it is little different from earlier historical works by scholars who never heard of social science but were sensitive to the multifarious aspects of human behavior. If we have discussed Dore and Wakeman here, it is, first, to show how the institutional pattern of training and support in area studies promotes this kind of writing; and second, to show the writing of history as it is. For all our discussion of antithetical ideal types in the first chapter above, historians and their work do not fit into neat boxes. There is social-scientific history of the "ideal" variety; but more often we have simply history, *tout court*, informed in greater or lesser degree by the insights of the social scientist.

OTHER AREAS OF INQUIRY AND OPPORTUNITY

As we noted at the beginning of this chapter, any effort to convey by means of examples the scope of social-scientific history would necessarily be invidiously selective. Some of the most exciting and rewarding work is going on in areas we can only mention in passing.

Take, for instance, the study of elections and electoral behavior. This is a field where quantitative analysis is obviously useful, not only to the scholar but also to the politician, so that the earliest reports and collections of election results go back to the beginning of democratic voting procedures. Richard Jensen, in an essay on "American Election Analysis," cites in this regard two contradictory interpretations of the contest between James Bowdoin and John Hancock in Massachusetts in 1787 which came out right after the election and offered breakdowns of the vote by occupation and interest.[16]

The scholarly analysis of election results in this country goes back, like so much other quantitative social science, to the work of Francis Walker of the United States Census Bureau in the 1870s and 1880s and to the historical seminar founded at the Johns Hopkins University at about the same time by Daniel Coit Gilman and Herbert Baxter Adams. The work begun there was continued by Frederick Jackson Turner, who trained two generations of historians and political scientists at Wisconsin (1885–1910) and Harvard (1910–24).

The Turnerian tradition of empirical, quantitative history—what Jensen calls the "Turnerian paradigm"—did not outlive its master. The historians who had initiated explorations in this sphere abandoned it to the political scientists, where it was married to the wave of behavioralism emanating from psychology and sociology. Why they did so is hard to say. The best explanation seems to be that they were more interested in other things; they also lacked the statistical training to stay on top of the material. The failure to impart such training, Jensen feels, was the greatest weakness of the Turnerian school.[17]

[16] Richard Jensen, "American Election Analysis: A Case History of Methodological Innovation and Diffusion," in S. M. Lipset, ed., *Politics and the Social Sciences* (Oxford: Oxford University Press, 1969), pp. 226–43.

[17] A similar shift of work in this area from history to political science took place in France, where the pioneer study was André Siegfried's *Tableau politique de la France de l'Ouest sous la IIIᵉ République* (1913).

Studies of electoral behavior tended to languish in the 1930s, when social scientists were busy responding to the depression and voting patterns were left more or less to the pollsters. After the war there was a revival, initiated in large part by V. O. Key and immensely stimulated by the adoption of computer technology. This last was the doorway to a new world of scholarship. What once had taken the most devoted researchers years of laborious calculation could now be done in a matter of weeks; and many things were now feasible that had been simply unthinkable before. A data bank like the Minnesota Political Data Archive, for example, is assembling machine-readable information on fifty countries, covering two dozen or more political variables and an equally catholic array of social and economic. The Inter-University Consortium for Political Research of the Institute for Social Research at the University of Michigan has acquired all of the major political surveys of the past twenty-five years and is collecting, both for the United States and foreign countries, on both the local and national level, all the election statistics, census data, and legislative records it can lay its hands on.[18] The exploitation by historians of the opportunities presented by these storehouses of information still lies in the future and will depend in large part on the extension to history students of the kind of statistical and methodological training now provided in the other social sciences. In the meantime, a number of pioneers, to some extent self-educated, have shown the way in computerized political history: Lee Benson, Richard Jensen, Joel Silbey, and others in United States history; William Aydelotte in the history of British politics of the nineteenth century; Patrice Higonnet in his studies of the France of 1789 and the Monarchie Censitaire (1814–48).

Social mobility is another area where the computer has enhanced enormously the possibilities of the researcher. Whereas once historians were confined to impressionistic inferences from contemporary opinion or a limited sample of careers, it is now feasible to process hundreds of biographies, verify the direction and extent of social mobility, and correlate with other variables. Whereas once the scholar was limited to preselected samples of "successful" men who had made it into biographical dictionaries, even such huge, "democratic" sources as censuses and street and telephone directories, once unmanageable, can now serve.[19] As a result the theses of so-

[18] Cf. Ralph L. Bisco, "Social Science Data Archives: Progress and Prospects," *Social Science Information*, VI (1967), 39–74.
[19] See Peter R. Knights, "City Directories as Aids to Ante-Bellum Urban

ciology and political science, as well as history, have been subject to refutation and revision: witness Stephan Thernstrom's *Poverty and Progress: Social Mobility in a Nineteenth-Century City* (1964), which offers a serious amendment to Lloyd Warner's earlier work on Newburyport (Yankee City).

One line of research opened up by the new techniques that has not yet been explored is the pursuit of mobility through the ramifications of the single case rather than by inference from a large number of cases. What, for example, have been the fortunes of a given family over a long period—not only the successful members, but all the members? To do this would require extensive genealogical research over many generations, research that would take a long time even for a family of moderate fecundity.[20] But such an approach, especially once the number of case studies had multiplied, would yield new insights into social mobility that all the macroanalyses in the world could not provide.

In particular, such family histories could be executed in depth, with due attention where possible to the details of intrafamilial relations and values. In this way they could provide the evidential basis for psychological as well as sociological analyses. They could in effect provide a bridge between individual case studies and the psychoanalysis of group behavior. Prosopography, which we discussed above for its contribution to our knowledge of the social and political history of antiquity, could serve a similar purpose. Perhaps no area of historical scholarship is so promising as this; yet none is so frustrating in its subtlety and intangibility.

Psychological and psychoanalytical history is still in its infancy. When, in 1957, William Langer chose to devote his presidential address to the American Historical Association to this topic, he called his talk "The Next Assignment." [21] In typical Langer fashion, he brought together an impressive array of bibliographical citations to

---

Studies: A Research Note," *Historical Methods Newsletter*, no. 2 (September, 1969), 1–10.

[20] Two examples of such genealogical censuses, though not presented or analyzed from the standpoint of social science, are the work of Arnaud Chaffanjon: *La Marquise de Sévigné et sa descendance* (Paris, 1962) and *Jean Racine et sa descendance* (Paris, 1964).

[21] William L. Langer, "The Next Assignment," *American Historical Review*, LXIII (1958); reprinted in his *Explorations in Crisis: Papers in International History* (Cambridge, Mass., 1969), pp. 408–32. See also Hans-Ulrich Wehler, "Zum Verhältnis von Geschichtswissenschaft und Psychoanalyse," *Historische Zeitschrift*, CCVIII (June, 1969), 529–54. Both articles offer superb bibliographical introductions to the literature.

earlier work in this field; but even so, almost the entire task lay ahead, for much of what passed as psychological history was as yet unpersuasive and hence uninfluential. Some of the fault lay with the audience: historians for whom Freud was someone people talked about, or heard of, but never read. Some lay with the would-be psychological and psychoanalytic historians, who were sometimes trained in psychology, sometimes in history, but rarely in both. And some lay with the subject matter, which was rarely intimate and explicit enough to permit serious exploration of psychic influences and behavior. If the psychoanalyst has as much trouble as he does with a live patient stretched out on his office couch, if even under such circumstances, psychiatry and psychoanalysis are as much art as science, how much more difficult and uncertain it is to apply this technique to history!

Yet psychohistory has continued to move forward on both the micro and macro levels, and there is growing evidence that we have now crossed beyond guesswork and inspiration to that region of replicative inquiry and verification where the gains are cumulative and genius is reinforced by hard work. On the level of personal analysis, the most exciting contributions have been those of Erik Erikson, which have served as prototypes for a growing body of biographical psychohistory.[22] Like all imitative responses, most of this work is inferior to that of the master. For one thing, Erikson came to history from psychiatry; few of his epigoni have had serious psychoanalytic training. For another, his stage model of personal development was derived from the experience of a Western, industrial, affluent society and would have to be modified for other places and times. Some of his followers have not taken this into account. Still, it is clear that the incorporation of psychic considerations into biographical analysis enriches enormously our understanding of human behavior; and that in the future, more of the practitioners of psychohistory will be trained in both fields. Their credentials may never entirely satisfy the members of either discipline—that is the hazard of all attempts to marry two competences—but they will meet the requirements of effective interdisciplinary work.

[22] Even historians who do not explicitly take Erikson's stage model as their model have been influenced by his thought. See, to take only one example, Michel Confino's "Histoire et psychologie: A propos de la noblesse russe au XVIIIᵉ siècle," *Annales: économies, sociétés, civilisations,* XXII (1967), 1163–1205. In this sense, Erikson has become part of the intellectual baggage of an increasing number of contemporary historians and, like Marx, Freud, or Weber, serves them as inspiration or antiinspiration.

On the macro level, studies of group psychological phenomena are increasingly frequent and are opening new areas of research that have up to now been ignored or taken for granted. One such area is the history of child-rearing, where Philippe Ariès' *Centuries of Childhood*, which covers almost a millennium in an impressionistic but most imaginative way, is now stimulating work of a more focused, scientific character.[23] Another is the psychoanalysis of social and cultural integration: see, for example, a fascinating essay by Georges Devereux on ancient Sparta.[24] Still another is social psychopathology: the response to natural disaster or pandemics, the rise of persecution manias, the behavior of mobs, the nature of totalitarianism. Some of the possibilities here are still latent rather than realized; recent psychological work on the therapeutic effects of participation in psychodrama have found frequent and even facile application to the analysis of riots and other forms of collective behavior in contemporary society but not as yet to historical instances. Yet it is now clear that no account of strike actions, street riots, and rebellions of the past can be complete unless it takes account of the psychological components: the exhilarating effects of risk and sacrifice, the warmth of togetherness, the euphoric surrender to faith, the female appeal to masculine virility, and the drive of the young to prove their manhood by violence. The response of the authorities and the "establishment" is equally susceptible of psychoanalysis.

Finally there is "Olympian" psychohistory—the analysis of entire cultures and civilizations over long periods. One of the most influential practitioners of this art-science has been Norman O. Brown, who has sought and found the essence of history in fears, repressions, and sublimations—for example, in the conquest of death by the denial of life, its alienation into "dead" forms like money, metals, cities, or writing.[25] In technique and approach, if not always in substance, this universal psychohistory is allied to similar "Olympian" analyses of contemporary society by Karen Horney, Erich Fromm, Herbert Marcuse, and assorted neo-Freudians and post-Freudians;

[23] The book originally appeared as *L'Enfant et la vie familiale sous l'Ancien Regime* (Paris, 1960). A new contribution to the subject is David Hunt, *Parents and Children in History; The Psychology of Family Life in Early Modern France* (New York and London, 1970). See also the papers presented to a conference on "Childhood and Youth in History," Clark University, March 19–20, 1970.

[24] "La psychanalyse et l'histoire: une application à l'histoire de Sparte," *Annales: économies, sociétés, civilisations*, XX (1965), 18–44.

[25] Norman O. Brown, *Life Against Death: The Psychoanalytical Meaning of History* (Middletown, Conn., 1959); also his *Love's Body* (New York, 1966).

and indeed by Freud himself, in *Civilization and Its Discontents*. Like these others, the Brownian approach is stunning in its sweep and imagery; but also like these others, it operates on so high a level that it does not begin to touch most of the issues that historians are concerned with; and it relies so heavily on intution and inspiration that as yet it hardly lends itself to verification, refutation, or application. Even so, all these macroanalysts have, by subjecting the very foundations of our culture to scrutiny and criticism, initiated a drastic revision of our sense of our own history and hence of our self-image. Some economic historians will no doubt go on "explaining" the rise of capitalism and industrial society simply in terms of the conventional economic factors—the development of trade, the production of agricultural surpluses, and the increase of population —but their readers will no longer be satisfied. And for similar reasons, no serious student of the effects of industrialization in the West will confine himself to the usual social and cultural consequences: increased mobility, urbanization, population growth, and changes in the political balance of power, both within industrial nations and between them and the rest of the world. The psychological consequences—of materialism, affluence, social ambition, speed, and change—have now entered Clio's house and established residence.

SOCIAL-SCIENTIFIC HISTORY

What do these diverse studies of revolution, ancient aristocrats, nineteenth-century railroads, changes in the birth rate, Chinese civil war, and elections have in common? Certainly not their specific topics, the periods involved, the sources used, or even the arguments they embody. They do, however, evince a characteristic way of asking and answering questions.

Three salient concerns characterize most (though not all) work in social-scientific history. The first is the effort to produce what we may call *collective history*, that is, history directly linking the recorded experiences of large numbers of persons or social units to patterns of behavior or change. (Even when the social-scientific historian focuses his attention on a particular person or group, this concern is implicit: he tries to explain his subject in terms derived from wider observations and thereby to reinforce or verify by the singular our knowledge of the general.) Collective biography of the variety now being done with Roman or British political elites does this. So does the historical study of social mobility in China or America. Much of historical demography has this character. A number of other lines of investigation just opening up lead in the same direction; the history of epidemics, for example, can be very effectively written from the systematically accumulated records of individual victims rather than from the general impressions of observers or the haphazard selection of scattered cases.

Second, the social-scientific historian tries to account for and understand these patterns of collective behavior in terms of theoretical concepts and models. To this end, he begins where possible with an explicit statement of assumptions, concepts, and hypotheses; and he relies on evidence that is reproducible, verifiable, and potentially refutable. The concepts and procedures employed commonly come from adjacent social sciences such as demography and economics. The generalizations and conclusions derived from the data, however, are characteristically historical in their emphasis on the time dimension and the relationship of phenomena to context. These findings, moreover, have a demythifying function. The stories of ancestral virtue and foreign wickedness are not the only legends that confront the historian. The study of man abounds in myths that need to be tested against the record of human experience. Demographic and economic history have shown what can be done along these lines; we can expect similar contributions from other branches of history as they begin to address themselves to the theses and problems of the social and behavioral sciences.

In this sense, history has as much to give to the other social sciences as they have to give to history. For one thing, other social scientists are no less credulous of "myths" than historians; if anything, they are more so because of their unfamiliarity with the historical evidence. It is the research of French historians of Quebec that now enables us to scrutinize and revise those sociological explanations of contemporary French Canada that find their *deus ex machina* in an alleged French-Canadian "backwardness." And it took Stephan Thernstrom's study of Newburyport in the nineteenth century to remind us that Lloyd Warner's Yankee City was not so Yankee as he imagined, or as his informants imagined. The best social scientists recognize the need for time perspective. In 1933, when Paul Lazarsfeld, the father of survey analysis, arrived in the United States from Germany, he set down, in a paper entitled "Principles of Sociography," four basic rules of procedure. The Third Commandment ran: "Contemporary information should be supplemented by information on earlier phases of whatever is being studied." Yet the rule is honored as much in the breach as in the observance. The same Paul Lazarsfeld, in a study of voting behavior in Elmira, New York, asked why the entire population, including the working class, voted Republican. Had he looked back to the pre-World War I years, he would have found that Elmira had once had an extremely active and successful Socialist movement. His question should have been: why does the working class of Elmira, which once voted Socialist, now vote Republican? Clearly, social scientists and historians have in this respect a common interest: they both need to know the past, and it is this that explains the striking convergence of their work. Yet if this is so, the chief burden of the search falls to the historian and he must learn to carry it.

The third salient characteristic of social-scientific history is its extensive reliance on comparison—not that pro-forma laying of parallel experiences side by side that often passes as comparative history, but the systematic, standardized analysis of similar social processes or phenomena (for example, slavery) in different settings in order to develop and test general ideas of how those processes or phenomena work. Comparative history in this sense is not new, but it has received a powerful impetus from the growing attention of historians to the generalizations of social and behavioral science; for without generalization, without models to test in a variety of contexts, there is no rationale for comparison.

These characteristics of research—aggregation, the marriage of theory and empiricism, and systematic comparison—do not exhaust the realm of social-scientific history, nor are they confined to it. In some areas, moreover, they are still goals to be attained rather than achieved standards. In the same way, one could enumerate other secondary shibboleths of history as social science: the reliance on quantification, the use of computers and other devices for mechanical data-processing, the association with investigators drawn from outside the historical profession, the emphasis on formal presentation of argument and hypothesis, the recourse to a technical vocabulary; but again, these are at best signs and are not congruent with this branch of the discipline. Furthermore, as we remarked earlier, few historians are either pure humanists or pure social scientists. Almost all combine something of both, in various and varying proportions. If this looseness of characterization and ambiguity of affiliation troubles some of our readers, there is little we can do about it. History is no different in this respect from most other disciplines, which have their own difficulties defining themselves, their methodology, and their membership.

4

THE ROLE AND NEEDS
OF INSTRUCTION

One reason why the importance of new interests and techniques of historical scholarship will grow with time is the progressive alteration of the character and balance of historical evidence. The corpus of reasonably precise and intimate quantitative data on all aspects of life and behavior is growing enormously as more and more phenomena are brought into the realm of measurement; where numbers are wanting, surveys are creating them. Today the historian of earlier periods who for one reason or another is not interested in or has no use for numbers, has always been able to eschew or ignore them on grounds of inaccuracy, inadequacy, or irrelevance. He can live without them and, generally speaking, so can his students.

Yet what is the historian of the future to do—of the next generation or the one after that? There will be less and less of his subject that is not susceptible of measurement, and even if he finds a nonquantitative corner, not all his students will. One has only to follow the history of one of the new growth industries, data archives, to see what is happening. The historian who wants to do American political, social, or even cultural history of the twentieth century is going to have to be able to use the machine-readable data, primary and secondary, that are being collected now. If he cannot, he will be cut off from a good part of the crucial evidence, certainly the "hardest" evidence. He can, of course, leave this kind of thing to others—to sociologists, say, of a historical bent. But then, what is left of history? A truncated residue?

Some of this is already happening. More and more of what is vital to us as historians is being done outside the discipline. Collective

74

biographies of the occupants of particular social and occupational statuses, studies of the social origins of elites, histories of political participation and behavior, economic history, demographic history, ethnic history, local history—all of these are areas in which much or most of the newest and most exciting research is taking place outside history proper. Courses in the other social sciences take on an increasingly historical cast; journals in the other social sciences print a significant number of articles of historical content; professors in the other social sciences produce history books and direct dissertations that are in fact historical investigations.

All of this is good for social science and for knowledge in general. But insofar as history finds itself cut off, or cuts itself off, from this growing body of scholarship and the source material it rests on, history is the poorer. It has always been the pride of the historian that he is the custodian and evaluator of primary historical evidence. It is the others, the theorists and generalizers of the other social sciences, who are content to rely on processed material and secondary sources. The historian cannot afford to abandon this task—not because it will fall to weak or unreliable hands, but because history cannot be critical and scientific unless it keeps this minimal function.

In short, the history student of today must learn social science statistics, computer techniques, model-building, and ancillary skills, if not for himself, then for his students. He has to learn these for the same reason that he learns foreign languages—because without them he cannot read the relevant literature and use the relevant sources.

THE CONTEXT

More than the other behavioral and social science fields, history has always been a teaching discipline. This is shown by enrollment statistics. Within American universities, the aggregate undergraduate course enrollment in history is more than half again as large per department as in the other social sciences: about 2,750 students as opposed to 1,600. The average history department awards about twice as many BA's each year (90) as the average department elsewhere in the social sciences (50). The same is true at the level of master's degrees: about 24 MA's per year in history, against 12 in the other social science departments. The disparity disappears only at the doctoral level; history departments award about 5 a year; other social science departments 4.[1] Interestingly enough, when allowance is made for the prestige ranking of the department (as given, for example, by the Cartter ratings), the distinction between the teaching obligations of history and other behavioral and social science departments still holds, and the disparity appears greatest in the most distinguished institutions.[2] In these, history departments outrank the others by nearly two to one in BA's, better than two to one in MA's, and once again, by a smaller margin in PhD's, as shown in Table 4-1. (The contrast here with the other social sciences appears strikingly in data assembled by the Office of Education, shown in Table 4-2.)

TABLE 4-1   AVERAGE NUMBER OF DEGREES GRANTED PER DEPARTMENT, 1965–66, BY CARTTER CATEGORY

Department	Distin- guished or Strong	Good or Adequate	Not Ranked (Low)	Not in Survey	Total Depart- ments
BA					
History	159[a]	92	73	58	89
Other soc sciences	86	62	41	27	50
Total soc sciences	100	69	46	33	57
MA					
History	46	23	21	13	24
Other soc sciences	19	13	10	8	12
Total soc sciences	24	15	11	9	14
PhD					
History	15	5	3	1	5
Other soc sciences	11	7	4	2	5
Total soc sciences	12	6	3	2	5

Source: Departmental questionnaire. Cartter categories based on those established in An Assessment of Quality in Graduate Education, by Allan M. Cartter (Washington, D. C.: American Council on Education, 1966).
[a] Numbers rounded to nearest integer.

[1] These and the following statistical statements about university departments of history are based on the findings of a survey of all social science departments in the United States granting the PhD conducted under the direction of the Behavioral and Social Sciences Survey Committee. Further technical information concerning this survey will be found in the Appendix of the overall report of the Survey Committee, The Behavioral and Social Sciences: Outlook and Needs (Englewood Cliffs, N. J.: Prentice-Hall, Inc., 1969).
[2] Prestige ratings from Alan M. Cartter, An Assessment of Quality in Graduate Education (Washington, D. C.: American Council on Education, 1966). Departments were characterized as distinguished, strong, good, adequate, and not ranked (low).

TABLE 4-2 DISTRIBUTION OF FACULTY WITHIN TEACHING FIELDS BY
LEVEL OF INSTRUCTION OFFERED (Aggregate United States, Spring, 1963)

Primary Teaching Field	Student Level Taught Most Frequently			
	Freshmen & Sophomores	Juniors & Seniors	Graduate Students	Other
History	60.0% (51.1)[a]	34.9% (41.8)	4.8% (6.6)	0.4 (0.5)
Anthropology	39.1 (33.8)	39.0 (39.2)	21.9 (27.0)	0.0 (0.0)
Economics	30.1 (21.3)	53.4 (55.6)	16.1 (22.6)	0.3 (0.5)
Political science and government	39.4 (32.5)	52.4 (56.6)	7.8 (10.3)	0.4 (0.5)
Sociology	30.9 (20.2)	54.8 (59.9)	14.4 (19.9)	0.0 (0.0)

Source: Ralph E. Dunham, Patricia S. Wright and Marjorie O. Chandler, *Teaching Faculty in Universities and Four-Year Colleges* (Washington, D. C.: U. S. Government Printing Office, 1966), Tables 11 and 12.
[a] The figures in parentheses show the proportion taught most frequently by doctorate-holders. (Figures may not add to 100 percent due to rounding.)

Whether this discrepancy will continue is, however, hard to say. There is some evidence, as we have seen, that undergraduates are shifting away from history to more "relevant" disciplines like sociology and political science. In the meantime, history remains the only social science that is required in many universities, often by state law, to furnish service courses to large numbers of undergraduates who must learn something about the history of their country or state in order to graduate. Further, the generalization of some form of history requirement in the elementary and secondary schools of most states implies the training of large numbers of history teachers at these levels, so that a good part of the graduate instruction in history is dispensed to elementary and high school teachers seeking additional subject-matter credits for advancement in their own systems. The large number of MA's in history is explained in part by this clientele.

All of these obligations, moreover, have made it necessary, possible, and profitable (in the pecuniary sense) for historians to write textbooks for all levels of instruction. Also, because the public interest in historical work is greater than in other forms of nonfiction, historians have always produced books, articles, and lectures for a large audience of nonprofessionals.

These obligations and opportunities are not a disadvantage. On the contrary, for many historians, teaching and popularization (the mission to the Philistines) are the most important and stimulating aspects of their work. This is particularly true if teaching: the one thing that just about all the members and informants of the Perkins-Snell Committee on Graduate Education of the American Historical Association could agree on was the importance of teaching and of teaching graduate students to teach. Many felt that the historical profession had neglected or depreciated teaching for the sake of research; even those whose primary interest was research argued that teaching and research are not competitive, but complementary, and that the pursuit of the one enhances the pursuit of the other.

Yet the two activities are competitive in one sense: they compete for the historian's time and attention. This is a fact that must be emphasized, without any invidious implications, because of its obvious consequences for the quantity and quality of original research. The ambiguous character of the historian's teaching responsibilities and opportunities for popularization is reflected in the responses to our individual survey. Many respondents, for example, not only stressed the importance of teaching but also expressed some fear that the emphasis on research is inimical to the best interests of the discipline. One of them, for example complained of:

> the aimless irrelevance of most of the work being done in both the humanities and the social sciences by America's scholars, and the increasing neglect of teaching in favor of research, and, finally, the emphasis placed on research as opposed to reflection.

Others tried to reconcile the two goals:

> I believe in the strong liberal arts program for undergraduates, including literature, classics, philosophy as well as *a* social science. As far as training in history is concerned, it seems more important that undergraduates learn to think as historians, to be concerned with the way historians work with their evidence and formulate their questions, than to cram facts. . . . Historical work requires uninterrupted and protracted periods of research

and writing. I believe the younger teachers should have lighter loads and adequate salaries to encourage use of such time without need to keep the wolf away by pot-boiling. Grad students need more secure fellowship tenures.

Many of our respondents, however, felt a direct conflict between their heavy teaching obligations and their active desire to investigate new problems. We asked them, for example, to indicate which of a long list of potential obstacles to research, in their own experience of the previous three years, had been major, minor, or insignificant hindrances to their work. Table 4-3 presents the answers they gave, according to the recency of the PhD. While nearly a third of the respondents named no major obstacle and administrative burdens were the largest single item cited,[3] two features of teaching—the overall load and the obligation to teach courses irrelevant to research interests—loomed together largest among the obstacles. More important, unlike administrative work, teaching burdened the younger scholars most: of the historians less than six years from their PhD, 36 percent named teaching load as the major obstacle to their research and 17 percent cited the need to teach subjects irrelevant to their research interests. Like the articulate minority who condemned their colleagues for sacrificing their true calling of teaching to research, the younger historians tend to see the problem as an irreconcilable conflict.

In our view both groups are wrong . . . or ought to be. At the extreme, it is true, total commitment to classroom teaching would leave no time for individual research and total commitment to individual research would leave no time for classroom teaching. Much of the apparent conflict, however, results from archaic and unexciting ideas of both activities. At present most history is taught in units that bear no relation to the teacher's own research. The standard course aims to fill a box in space and time—seventeenth-century England, colonial America, Ch'ing China—a box that comprises any number of topics and problems with which the teacher has little familiarity and even less concern. Such courses have their virtues, at least in principle: it is good for students of history to try to encompass the wholeness of a given society in a given period; moreover teaching such a course is an education in itself, if—and that's

---

[3] This is one load that is almost sure to increase as the result of current efforts to restructure the university.

TABLE 4-3 OBSTACLES TO RESEARCH, BY YEAR OF PhD (by percentage listing obstacle as "major")

Potential obstacle	No Answer	Before 1945	1945 to 1956	1957 to 1962	After 1962	Total
Excessive university administrative responsibility	36%	28%	40%	30%	12%	28%
Excessive teaching load	27	18	26	30	36	28
Lack of funds for research	9	15	18	18	17	17
Excessive outside work or writing commitments	9	15	21	12	7	14
Lack of research assistance	0	11	14	10	15	12
Weakness of university library	27	7	10	9	15	11
Organization of libraries, archives, data depositories	9	6	7	14	15	10
Need to teach subjects irrelevant to research	0	3	5	14	17	10
Inadequate leave arrangements	18	7	6	16	6	9
Weakness of local data-handling facilities	9	3	2	3	3	3
Other	9	12	10	6	4	8
None	46	33	26	30	36	31
Number of persons responding	11	108	171	139	144	573

Source: Special survey of historians in twenty-nine history departments (see Appendix).

a big *if*—the instructor makes a real effort to grasp the totality of his subject.

Yet for many historians, especially the social-scientific ones, and for an increasing number of students, the conventional unit is unsatisfactory and unsatisfying, in that it fails to focus on the kind of analytical problem that transcends time and place and must be studied and taught in a comparative context. The man who works on elites and power, or the growth of cities, or social unrest, or population change, wants to, and should, teach courses that treat of such topics as he sees them from the vantage point of his own research. This may not be all that he should teach, but insofar as he can talk about what he is doing—the topics that "turn him on"— he can communicate as in no other area the excitement of the search for knowledge and the rewards of discovery. This approach, moreover, as no other, makes it possible to convey to his students the hazards of that most perilous yet most unavoidable of historical maneuvers—the leap from the particular to the general. Historians have long warned themselves and their students of the pitfalls of generalization; some would have us eschew it entirely in view of the ontological uniqueness of every person and every event. Yet in fact there is more untidy generalization in most conventional time-space courses than a diligent scholar can verify or refute in a lifetime. If courses were more closely related to first-hand research, even the most ambitious, wide-ranging comparative research, they would be more critical and circumspect in this regard.

History teaching is moving in this direction, but very slowly. The historian who proposes not only to study peasant life, but also to teach courses on peasants is both rare and suspect. Although recent historical research has rearranged our general understanding of industrialization, it is nearly impossible to introduce the study of industrialization as such into the historical curriculum. Even the designers of courses in Black History, with all their desire to innovate, seem to have accepted the prevailing notion that a basic history course consists of the experience of a particular population in a particular area over a specific span of time. Why shouldn't it be the historical study of different patterns of race relations, the comparison of the American civil rights movement and its successors with previous movements of protest and power, the investigation of what happened to different groups of Africans as they spread throughout the world? As it is, the training of young historians, the implicit commitment young and old historians alike have made to their various publics, and the ponderous historical curricula of schools and colleges all conspire against such definitions of the subject matter.

It is here that the service obligations of the profession become most costly. The need to offer courses to meet the interests of "outsiders," combined with all the other commitments on the elementary or popular level, means that most teachers of history have the satisfaction of talking about what absorbs their imaginations—their own research—only to the smallest of their many audiences, their most advanced students. Nothing is better calculated to insure that the newest, freshest, most promising avenues of research will have the most meager reception. Nothing could better guarantee that outmoded but conventional doctrine will persist long beyond its usefulness. Nothing could make it more certain that students will trudge away from their history courses unaware of their relevance to intellectual, moral, and political questions of the present day.

CURRENT GRADUATE TRAINING IN HISTORY

Undergraduate education in history consists almost exclusively in the introduction of the student to the substantive knowledge of history itself; graduate education, overwhelmingly so. Indeed, it is no exaggeration to say that of all the social sciences, none is less introspective about the way it does its work. There are some historians, even, who look upon a concern with methodology as a kind of intellectual "cop-out"—a refuge for those who cannot write good history.

As a result, methodology is the orphan of the history curriculum. At the time of the Snell report (1956–58), one in three colleges was offering a course in methodology; the same held true for historiography. There is no reason to believe that these proportions have altered since. Most of this instruction consists of reading "Greats" and discussion, on the broadest, most conventional level, of the philosophical and epistemological basis of historical knowledge. Of explicit training in research design, quantitative methods, and the theory of related disciplines, there is almost nothing, so that many of the most significant and exciting recent contributions to history—in regard to the family, immigration, economic growth, mass movements, demographic change, urbanism, and similar themes—have been the work of exceptional persons who have somehow risen above their own education.

Even from the point of view of "traditional history," however, present methods of historical training leave much to be desired. Problems concerning the design of research, the logical requirements of proof, the drawing of inferences from documents, or the imaginative use of new kinds of evidence—are by no means peculiar to any one kind of history. They are standard problems in the logic of research—any kind of research—and they are as relevant to the quality of the work done in "traditional" history as they are to more interdisciplinary forms of historical inquiry. Even so, as our survey has disclosed, such general considerations of the logic of investigation are no more a standard part of the "training" of graduate students than more sophisticated attempts to make use of social theory and new research methods. Those schools that offer courses in methodology do not always require their graduate students to take them. Instead, the student is either assumed to have had this kind of instruction at some earlier stage or is left to his own devices; he is expected to learn how to write history by reading history (just as he is expected to learn how to teach by sitting in front of teachers and watching them at work). Even courses in what we may call the varieties of history (sequences of topics representative of different aspects of historical change—diplomatic, political, social, religious, and so forth), increasingly popular and required at a number of graduate schools of all incoming history students, focus primarily on the substance of the topics treated. The methods used by the authors of the smorgasbord of readings offered are noted in passing and the student is left to absorb some kind of lesson in the process.

In short, it would hardly be an exaggeration to say that most graduate students in history are given no "training" at all. For the most part, the drill seems to be the mastery of certain pieces of knowledge, defined in a traditional way, and the writing of a thesis —again usually defined in a traditional way—in which all methodological and conceptual problems are felt to be soluble by the application of "common sense." The body of knowledge for which the student is held responsible (on oral examinations, for example) is in most instances defined in terms of some combination of time and space: the Colonial Period of American History, English History in 1485, the History of France from 1660 to 1789. Most doctoral theses, moreover, follow the same pattern. This method of instruction can claim impressive accomplishments at its best, but there seems little doubt that it now acts as a drag upon the training of scholars in fields that require conscious—and conscientious—concern for problems of method and the use of concepts not usually met with in history courses. Indeed, this method of instruction, as presently practised, seems inadequate even for the training of the kind of historian it was designed to produce, since its effect is to cut off both professors and students from wide areas of exciting and significant intellectual activity.

This impoverishment is aggravated, moreover, by the insistence of many historians on treating their discipline as intellectually self-sufficient. There is some justification for this in the intrinsic scope of the subject; after all, all aspects of man and his behavior are grist for the historian's mill, and in principle, the historian should be prepared to learn whatever techniques or concepts are required to evaluate and understand his data. In fact, the statistics make clear the excessively inward character of the discipline, with a special weakness on the side of social science. Of our sample of historians, for example, 71 percent majored in history as undergraduates, while another 16 percent majored in some branch of the humanities; that left only 13 percent from all other fields. When asked whether they had "substantial formal training" in subjects outside of history, the historians responded as shown in Table 4-4.

The figures shown in fig. 4-1 are confirmed by data produced by a general survey of the National Academy of Sciences, covering field

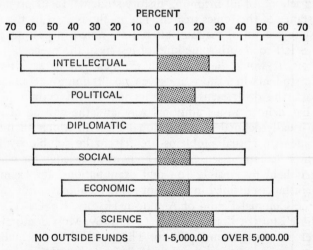

FIGURE 4-1 PERCENTAGE OF HISTORIANS CLAIMING "SUBSTANTIAL" TRAINING IN VARIOUS FIELDS

Data from Special Survey of Historians (see Appendix B).

TABLE 4-4 APPLICATIONS, ADMISSIONS AND FINANCIAL AIDS, NEWLY ENTERING GRADUATE STUDENTS, AUTUMN 1967

	Anthropology	Economics	Geology	History	Linguistics	Political Science	Psychology	Sociology
Number of students who applied for admission	3,350	11,251	1,920	17,276	1,571	12,875	30,295	778
Percentage of students accepted	47	46	62	49	56	45	21	43
Percentage of applicants actually enrolled	26	20	39	22	32	21	11	21
Percentage requesting financial aid	78	73	84	72	33	77	88	78
Percentage of applicants offered aid	16	15	21	13	17	13	11	16
Percentage of those accepted offered aid	33	32	45	26	30	28	50	39
Average stipend per receiving student	$3081	$3189	$3013	$2767	$3519	$2917	$3065	$3090

Source: *The Behavioral and Social Sciences: Outlook and Needs* (see Appendix).

changes from the baccalaureate to the doctorate and the master's
degree to the doctorate in 1958–66. In that period, only 9 percent
of history PhD diplomates showed a social science undergraduate
major (66 percent had majored in history); and only 4 percent of
masters (as against 76 percent from history).

As we have seen, the degree to which historians show evidence of
formal training outside their discipline is a function of their specialties. There are some areas of history in which this kind of outside training is almost indispensable, economic history for example,
and the statistics reflect this complementarity. Even in these areas,
however, we find less instruction outside of history than we would expect: thus of the forty-four historians in our sample who reported
economic history as their principal field of competence, only twenty-
seven declared "substantial" training in economics. What is perhaps
more worrisome, the self-identified social historians reported the least
outside training of any kind, including training in the social sciences.
The implication would seem to be that this, more than other areas
of specialization, is one in which technical training is not felt to
be necessary and the common-sense conventional techniques are
somehow deemed adequate.

This parochialism of background is bad enough in itself; but it is
compounded by an unawareness of or indifference to the problem. A
survey by the Perkins-Snell committee of 182 history PhD's of 1958
showed that only 4 percent thought that their undergraduate preparation in the humanities and social sciences was "greatly inadequate."
And the Perkins-Snell report itself hardly touches the question of interdisciplinary training on the graduate level.[4] As a result, although
most history departments have come to admit the *possibility*, perhaps even *desirability*, of including an outside field among the three,
four, or five fields that must be prepared for the customary general
examination, very few have gone so far as to admit the *necessity* of
such outside training for those historians whose specialization would
seem to call for it. It continues, therefore, to be standard operating
procedure to turn out economic historians who have not done a field

[4] The chapter on "Major Criticisms of Ph.D. Training" deals with the following topics: preparation for teaching, breadth vs. specialization (primarily
within history proper), training for research and writing, and the time required
to complete the program. The need for outside fields is disposed of in two
sentences: "Many college respondents would like all Ph.D. candidates in history
to study in at least one related discipline. Graduate faculty members for the
most part agree that one outside field is desirable." Dexter Perkins and John L.
Snell, *The Education of Historians in the United States* (New York: McGraw-
Hill Book Company, 1962), pp. 169–70.

in sociology. Almost no departments have arrived as yet at a conception of their subject flexible enough to admit the possibility that a doctoral candidate might offer half or even more than half of his fields in outside disciplines and still think of himself, by training, field of interest, and predilection, as a historian.

In the meantime, there are departments like that at Harvard that continue to insist that all candidates for the doctorate take one of their fields (in this case one out of four) in some specified area of history (in this case ancient or medieval). The justification for such requirements is laudable: that it is desirable and intellectually broadening to introduce students to eras and populations very different from those on which they will concentrate their efforts. Yet this is, by implication, an extremely invidious and condescending attitude. Is there something about sociology or political science that makes these subjects somehow less broadening to a student of history—of any kind and any period?

The same inflexibility shows itself in the language requirements for the PhD degree. The standard requirement of two foreign languages (more, of course, in many areas of history) is well-nigh universal, no matter what the area of general interest of the student and no matter what kind of historical work he proposes to do. It is not our intention here to deprecate this requirement or to propose that historians can afford to sacrifice this tool of their profession. There is no doubt that knowledge of foreign languages makes for a better-educated man, and what is more to the point for our purposes, that only with considerable linguistic training can historians do the kind of comparative history that we advocate here. Yet there are languages and languages; for different historians, some take priority over others. Mathematics and statistics are also languages, as are computer programs; it may well be more important and urgent for a graduate student in social-scientific history to learn these things first, before his second foreign language and maybe even before his first, in order to graduate from student to scholar. What we are suggesting, in other words, is not a reduction in the requirement, but an expansion that adds new languages to the list; and a loosening of priorities so that these new languages may be taken in the most appropriate order.

To complete this picture of the character of graduate training in history, it should be noted that history students, in spite of these limitations on the scope of their preparation, do not complete their doctorates any faster than others. If anything, they take slightly longer. At the same time, they receive less financial aid: history stands lowest of all social sciences in the percentage of newly enrolled students to whom aid is extended (political science stands at the same low level) and in the average stipend offered per entering student. This relative impoverishment persists throughout the degree program. A survey of graduate students in the arts and sciences prepared by Joe L. Spaeth of the National Opinion Research Center of the University of Chicago for the American Historical Association shows that historians have fewer sources of stipendiary support (fellowship or teaching or research assistantship) than even the impecunious humanists, let alone the social scientists and natural scientists. Only 12 percent of the historians in the sample were able to support themselves with some kind of assistantship, as against 22 percent of the humanists, 20 percent of the social scientists, and over one third of the natural scientists.[5] Putting assistantships and fellowships together, we find a third of the historians financed in this way, against almost half of the humanists and social scientists and three quarters of the natural scientists. If we count partial as well as full support, we have 52 percent of the historians holding a stipend, 62 percent of the humanists, 65 percent of the social scientists, and 80 percent of the natural scientists.[6] Such stipends as the historian does receive, moreover, are substantially smaller than those in the other disciplines: historians are the only group, for example, more than half of whose fellowships do not cover more than tuition, in whole or in part. Perhaps because their expectations match their real chances, historians ask for less support: the survey showed that the proportion of disappointed applications was about the same for all fields. The history student, in other words, is realistically inured to deprivation.

How does the history student pay his way? More often than in other fields, he takes an outside job, often a full-time job. Such jobs, by comparison with the full-time employments of students in the social and natural sciences, are not well paid: about 30 percent of them paid over $4,500 a year, as against 50 percent in the biological sciences, slightly over 50 percent in the social sciences, and 70 percent in the physical sciences. The history student also has somewhat more put by in the form of savings or investments and he borrows more than students in other fields. All of this is not without

[5] Joe L. Spaeth, unpublished (mimeographed) report, National Opinion Research Center (Chicago: University of Chicago, n.d. [1960?]), p. 37, Table 2.
[6] Ibid., p. 38, Table 3a.

its psychological wear and tear: the same survey shows historians and humanists to be the most worried and least optimistic about their immediate financial situation and their long-run futures.

Inadequate support also has its intellectual price. What the historian gives to his outside job, he must take from his preparation as scholar and teacher; and even if he earns his money teaching, the nature of his assignment is often such as to constitute a diversion from the real business of his education. Learning the techniques and substance of his own specialty, let alone those of related disciplines, will have to be deferred to some indefinite later time, when he has his diploma and his job and maybe even tenure. By then he usually finds that he has acquired new commitments and has less time than ever for his good intentions.

The inadequacy of financial support is similarly reflected in the individualistic character of graduate research. In the other social sciences, support comes more often than not from some larger project that groups a number of students, working separately or severally, in some common inquiry. Often the project has a physical location that makes it possible for the members, both students and faculty, to meet, talk, and learn from one another at work. History offers nothing comparable. The nearest equivalent would be the opportunity for some historians to find good intellectual company in area centers. But these, we have seen, are usually confined to studying the more exotic parts of the globe. The great mass of historians are to be found in the more conventional fields of American and European history, and here this kind of intellectual cum physical propinquity is almost invariably lacking. Such scholarships as are available are awarded individually, and it is as individuals that the students pursue their research. If serious progress is to be made in the imparting of a larger interdisciplinary bundle of techniques to students in history, some way must be found to increase the kind of peer-group communication that is characteristic of the other social sciences.

To sum up: present methods of graduate instruction in history assume the creation of a particular type of historian and, therefore, of a particular type of history. That historian is one who is broadly knowledgeable in the substance of a number of times and places; more or less competent in foreign languages (one could write a book about the credibility gap here); proficient in the technical analysis of documents; and particularly responsive to the work of scholars in literature, art history, and political theory. He is not ordinarily responsive to the substance of knowledge or research procedures developed in the other social sciences; does not have the conceptual tools needed to produce truly comparative history; lacks the quantitative techniques needed to control the large masses of data indispensable to the analysis of many problems in social history; and lacks the knowledge of both economic and social theory and of research methods that would allow him to undertake historical research designed to test the adequacy of existing theory or to add to existing theory.

RECOMMENDATIONS FOR HISTORICAL TRAINING

Our purpose is not to assert the claims of one type of historian or the superiority of one type of history over another. It is to recognize, first, the legitimacy of many modes of historical inquiry; to assert that the advancement of history is furthered by a definition of the discipline broad enough to encompass these modes; and to urge that the profession live and work by that definition— by providing a climate of hospitality for those who wish to innovate in historical research as well as for those who wish to assert their mastery over traditional forms. Second, we want to emphasize that many of the ills noted above are by no means limited to those students of history who would work in social science; but that on the contrary, the entire discipline suffers from these constraints on the intellectual opportunities offered our students. It has long been taken for granted that a well-trained historian is familiar with areas of time and space beyond those of his own specialization, indeed that such breadth of knowledge is indispensable to intelligent work on even the most confined topic. By the same token, it is now obvious that all historians, in differing degree, must be offered a more varied, more interdisciplinary spectrum of instruction and training.

Realizing the promise of social-scientific history will require changes in the methods and organization of professional training. Some of the changes we have in mind actually revive older procedures that haven't fallen into disuse, while others break sharply with current practice. All of them offer considerable possibilities for the enrichment of undergraduate education. Our discussion of reforms, however, will concentrate on the graduate level. Before we discuss specific changes, let us state our immediate objectives:

1. Explicit and systematic instruction, including extensive participation by students themselves, in problems of research design, formulation of hypotheses, logical requirements of proof, and the selection of appropriate research techniques.

2. Systematic exposure of the student to the substantive findings, conceptual frameworks, and research methods of the other social sciences that seem promising for the understanding of history or that need modification in the light of historical knowledge. The problem is twofold: (a) What contribution can the systematic use of social theory make to the understanding of history? (b) How can historical knowledge aid in the development of social theory by providing evidence for the testing of existing theory and by suggesting new problems for investigation?

3. Involvement of students in the creation, collection, and interpretation of sources that are especially valuable in the study of problems of social-scientific history but are often ignored in traditional work. In part, this entails the imaginative search for existing, but ignored, sources; in part, it implies the creation by the historian of the very data he needs to carry out his inquiry.

To achieve these ends, we offer the following recommendations:

Changes in Curriculum

Departments of history should introduce into the curriculum a substantially larger number of courses defined by themes and problems (war, revolution, power, urbanization, agrarian society, for example), alongside the traditional courses that treat of units of space and time (such as the United States after 1865, Europe since 1815, Renaissance Europe).

In order to facilitate the introduction of such courses, colleges and universities should be prepared to encourage collaborative instruction by staff drawn from more than one discipline. This implies a readiness to cross-list courses in the departments concerned, or—if cross-listing is not appropriate—to lend staff for the purpose. If teaching obligations in the lending department make such transfers of faculty time difficult without compensation, universities should be prepared to finance these "borrowings."

Departments of history should, like the other social sciences, recognize the status of mathematics, statistics, and computer programs as languages; and should, where desirable, oblige students to learn these *in addition to* the foreign languages conventionally required, in such order as is appropriate to the students' need.

Departments of history should not only permit students to do part of their work in related disciplines, but should also require those students working on interdisciplinary problems (in fields like economic or social history, for example) to take the appropriate training outside of history. Graduate students should be permitted to do up to half their fields in other disciplines (as against the one outside field typically permitted at present) and should be exempted from those distribution requirements that make it impossible to undertake serious training outside history without sacrificing preparation in the area or areas of principal interest. (A student of modern European social history, for example, should not have to give up a field in sociology or modern Germany in order to satisfy a requirement that he do at least one field in premodern history.)

New Teaching Arrangements

The Seminar. No innovation in the modern history of higher education is more important than the seminar. This is, as most readers of this report already know, a class whose primary purpose is to offer the student training and practice (both are important) in research and writing. In principle, seminars are small (ten students or less), because the work calls for close supervision by the teacher and active round-the-table discussion within the group. In fact, under the pressure of student numbers, seminars have become in some universities a kind of bastard hybrid of the lecture course and the discussion course. Enrollments number in the dozens (we have heard of "seminars" with over seventy students) and the only similarity to the true seminar is that each student is required to do some kind of term paper. (Also—a negative resemblance—there is no final examination.)

This alteration of the character of the seminar is in part a response to recent increases in the size of the graduate student population, in part just another example of careless nomenclature. Yet it is also a logical consequence of a persistent erosion of the original purpose and character of the seminar as a teaching institution. In the beginning the seminar was intended to be, for the humanistic disciplines, what the laboratory has been for the natural sciences, that is, a kind of shop in which teacher and students would work and learn side by side. The ancestor of American history seminars, as introduced at the Johns Hopkins University in the 1870s, provided the kind of physical environment implied by this procedure: the seminar had quarters of its own, a library of its own, and space for students and teachers to work together in and out of class hours. Membership in the seminar was not a brief or evanescent experience, covering a quarter, or a term, or even two quarters, but a continuing experience covering several years and taking the student from apprenticeship to doctorate. The result was the publication of a series of monographs, sponsored by the seminar, that constitutes to this day a landmark in American historiography.

Such a seminar is not something that can be reproduced at will. It calls for a very different kind of commitment by both faculty and students from that which prevails today. In so far as the right people can be found, however (and there are many of them in the historical profession), the seminar-workshop offers the promise of better training, more productive and significant scholarship, and the development of the kind of rapport between teacher and student that seems too often to be wanting. We recommend, therefore, that departments of history:

1. Provide funds and facilities for the establishment of continuing seminars comparable to the teaching laboratories of the natural sciences, with desk and office space for students and staff, attached libraries for the collection and use of books and research materials, and provisions for the publication of the work of their members. The requirements of such a seminar would naturally vary with the subject, but it seems reasonable to estimate space requirements for offices, library, student work space, storage, and research services at about 2,000 square feet and a budget for operation (net of faculty salaries and student fellowships) of about $25,000 a year. This would include salaries for secretarial help and a librarian-archivist, office expenses, and funds for acquisitions, photocopy work, reproduction, and the like. It would not cover the initial costs of establishment, including core library and equipment outlays; travel expenses for participants, including some visitors; or the cost of special acquisitions.

2. Provide financial support for student members of such seminars in the form of regular fellowships and travel grants.

3. Provide space and funds for team teaching, with staff drawn from without as well as within the discipline.

4. Use such seminars as teaching units for undergraduate courses. In this way students and faculty could collaborate in instruction and profit from one another's experience far more effectively than under present magisterial arrangements. Also this would go a long way towards solving one of the greatest shortcomings of present-day graduate education: the lack of systematic training and practice in the art of teaching.

5. Insofar as circumstances permit, open such seminars to faculty and students from other universities.

These recommendations, it should be recognized, do entail certain risks. If these seminars proved as effective and attractive as we think they would be, they would pose the danger of the Balkanization of history departments into smaller, semiautonomous fiefs that could act as an impediment to just the kind of intellectual interchange and communication that we have been advocating throughout this report. Precautions would have to be taken, therefore, to insure that students can make a free and informed choice of seminars; can study in more than one, insofar as time permits; and can transfer when necessary from one to another without undue loss of time and work. In addition, provision must be made for those students whose tastes and subjects dispose them toward working alone rather than in groups and for those students for whom seminar arrangements are not available. Finally, students should be required to take, as now, a substantial portion of their training outside their special field, hence outside their home seminar.

Note that although we are urging the creation of these workshop-seminars in the context of the development of social-scientific history, there is nothing in this proposal that confines their scope. Such seminars would be equally appropriate and, we are convinced, equally successful in other areas of history, which should also move in this direction. Otherwise there could well develop within a department an imbalance between programs of unequal drawing power.

Training in Method. In view of the increasingly esoteric and technical character of social-scientific research procedures, students of history can no longer substitute the traditional combination of common sense and self-education for systematic preparation. We therefore recommend that departments of history offer formal courses in historical method that include discussion of the appropriate literature of the other social sciences and practical training in the use and comprehension of quantitative data; that specialists be coopted from the other social sciences to share in this instruction; and that teaching materials explicitly addressed to the problems characteristic of historical research be developed for this purpose.

The last is particularly important. While a student of history can derive considerable benefit from a general course in statistics, such a course will not be able to provide extensive training in the kinds of statistical problems that are peculiarly characteristic of the spotty and imperfect data inherited from the past. Sometimes these short-comings impose severe constraints and limit the quantitative historian to rather elementary procedures, but at other times they yield to more sophisticated procedures than those learned in a typical statistics course. It is not, therefore, a question of developing easier courses for historians, but rather of developing courses explicitly adapted to their needs.

In addition to these improvements in the "higher training" offered history students, we should like to recommend that departments of history devote some attention to the "lower" techniques of note-taking, copying, photography, cartography, chart-making, and the like. Here again custom has left these matters to accident, idiosyncrasy, and trial-and-error, with the result that historians have been slow to take advantage of the efficiencies and opportunities available. All of these techniques have changed drastically over the past decade, while new conceptions of the scope of historical scholarship have enhanced their role considerably (thus, the use of photography in social history).

It goes without saying that a number of these recommendations cannot easily be carried out by small schools or departments. Some way must be found to make training like this available to larger numbers of students. To this end, we would urge schools and foundations to collaborate in increasing the number and variety of already existing summer programs and institutes providing instruction in mathematics and social science and other forms of specialized technical training for history graduate students. In a similar spirit, we recommend an expansion of the still exceptional practice of temporarily attaching students who need practical experience or technical training not available at their home institutions to teachers, seminars, museums, research institutes, and other facilities elsewhere. Such sojourns should become a regular and creditable part of graduate education. Major centers of demographic research, for example, could regularly take on a small number of apprentices for six months or a year at a time, simultaneously employing them in tasks for which they were suited and training them in demographic analysis and the handling of quantitative data. Regular exchange relationships between American universities and institutions in the countries in which the American students were specialized—for example, sending students from the University of Texas to work in a major professor's seminar at the University of Berlin, and vice versa—would accomplish some of the same objectives. Such exchanges, both within and outside the United States, could also become a regular feature of the workshop seminars proposed above. To be sure, all exchanges of this kind imply the possibility of a brain drain problem. Students may tend to gravitate to a few stronger schools at the expense of their home institutions. It is our conviction, however, that any such imbalance would be short-lived, and that the return of such trainees to their home universities, in combination with the normal dispersion effect of the academic marketplace, is in the long run the best assurance that new research methods and results will spread quickly and that smaller colleges and universities will have the knowledge and connections to attract talent. The effect will be the stronger if support is forthcoming from similar programs of visits by faculty members to workshops, centers, and the like at other institutions (see Chapters 5 and 6 below).

Finally, we recommend that universities make regular provision for the appointment (full-time or part-time) of mathematicians, statisticians, computer specialists, and other technical specialists to departments of history, for the specific purposes of providing individual and group instruction, offering advice on research procedures, providing liaison with major research facilities outside the department, and organizing local facilities for technical research.

Undergraduate Instruction. Some of the recommendations we have made for graduate education are directly applicable to undergraduate instruction; others, less so. Our argument in favor of the reorganization of lecture courses in history so as to reduce the number of courses ordered around conventional frameworks of time and space is equally valid at both the graduate and undergraduate levels. The more technical and specialized recommendations concerning the seminar and related institutions are, obviously, less appropriate to undergraduate education. The introduction of social-scientific approaches into the undergraduate curriculum will bring it new life, both because teachers will again be able to teach what absorbs them most and because students will more easily grasp the connections between historical problems and problems of the contemporary world. In any case, we feel strongly that the first serious exposure of history students to quantitative analysis and to the other social sciences should not wait upon their entering graduate school. We recommend that departments of history urge their undergraduate majors to take courses in statistics and in the other social sciences, and we would hope that in so far as history departments begin to *require* some training in statistics of their graduate students, undergraduates will find it advisable to acquire this training before entering graduate school, perhaps as partial satisfaction of a science distribution requirement.

General Financing

As the above-cited survey makes clear, history graduate students are not only underfinanced but also have learned to accommodate their expectations to their opportunities. They get little help and ask for little, and after a while, it is hard to say which comes first, the poverty or the small expectations. One of the most flagrant inequities in this regard is the arbitrary decision of the National Science Foundation, a major source of support for work in social science, to reject fellowship applications from history students regardless of their subject and methods; thus, two men can be working in the same area of history of science or economic history, and the one applying from a department of the history of science or economics will be eligible for aid, while the man from history will receive a small ready-printed rejection slip. In an effort to redress the situation, we recommend that both the government agencies and the private foundations allocate increased amounts for graduate fellowships in history and that such agencies as the National Science Foundation recognize their obligation to scholarship rather than labels and provide support for historical work that falls within the scope and satisfies the criteria of social science.

5
HISTORICAL RESEARCH AND POSTDOCTORAL TRAINING

THE PROBLEM

More historians are adopting social-scientific approaches to their work than are teaching them effectively or have an opportunity to teach them. Still more historians, however, face frustration in their desire to expand their knowledge and use of the social sciences. The constraints of the job and organization of the profession block the way. To take a glaring example: economic historians who have received their basic education in departments of history now turn away from important problems—the origins of the world depression of the 1930s, say, or the interlocking of imperialism and international trade—because they know too little of the economics involved, cannot learn the economics on their own, cannot afford to take the time required for new training, cannot enlist adequate assistance or collaboration, and cannot get support for the complex and expensive research involved. Worse yet, historians in general are shying away from economic history, which they are increasingly inclined to see as an arcane specialization of number-bound technicians. As a result, both history and economics are losers, for the historian brings to the subject advantages of erudition and perspective that complement the special virtues of the economist.

Economic history is, to be sure, a particularly obvious example of the intellectual isolation of the historian from a piece of his own subject. Yet the problem exists in other areas: ask the scholar who has not been trained in social science but realizes that in order to understand social mobility in the United States, he ought to know something about it in other contexts; the Latin American historian who wants to examine the connections among population growth, urbanization, and religious practice; the medieval historian concerned with kinship patterns; or the student of Nazi Germany who finds that he has to learn something about the psychopathology of the authoritarian personality. The historian whose interests are primarily methodological has almost no hope at all. The intelligent pursuit of social-scientific history often requires continuing technical education, considerable funds in new forms of support, interdisciplinary collaboration, and substantial research facilities.

All kinds of historians, of course, would be happy to enjoy these advantages—as our survey showed. Outside of social-scientific history and the history of science, however, most historians have long done without them, and with relatively little complaint; some have even made a virtue of their absence. It is the historians in the social-scientific specialties who feel these needs most acutely; and insofar as other historians expressed an interest in additional training, they showed a marked preference for work in social science. For example, we asked our sample of historians which of a long list of subjects they would take up in a summer institute, and again, which in a year's special training. The list stressed the social sciences, but included archaeology, philosophy, languages, physical sciences, and the option of some other subjects or none at all. Three quarters of our respondents expressed interest in a summer institute; two thirds, in a year's training. For the first group, 83 percent elected one of the social sciences, with sociology and statistics the favorite subjects. For those who would have liked a year's training, 75 percent chose a social science, with sociology and economics the most frequent choices. Economic, social, and diplomatic historians of Asia, Africa, Latin America, and (more surprisingly) the United States expressed considerably greater interest in such additional training than their colleagues in European history. The same general pattern holds for concern about research facilities, dissatisfaction with present fellowship arrangements and so on.

The interest, in other words, is great. We ought, therefore, to ask how existing arrangements for postdoctoral training, research, support, interdisciplinary collaboration, and the acquisition and organization of facilities for research could be revised to meet the growing and important demand.

FURTHER EDUCATION IN OTHER
SOCIAL SCIENCES

For all we have said about the promising application of anthropological or economic ideas and procedures in historical research, they cannot simply be ripped from their contemporary context and applied indiscriminately to other times, places, and materials. Historical evidence is frequently different in character—sometimes richer, sometimes poorer, but regularly different—from the evidence anthropologists or economists are used to handling. Furthermore, just as the sociological student of North American cities has to work hard to adjust his analyses to Lima or Buenos Aires, he has even a larger chasm to cross between himself and classical Rome. The transfer takes adaptation of concepts, methods, and styles of analysis.

The skills to effect this transfer are rare. Few people in history and in the other social sciences have sufficient interest and competence in other disciplines to do the work gracefully and intelligently. Eventually we shall train students up to the task. In the meantime, many of the historians now most interested in the social sciences are already past graduate school, while many of the coming generation will recognize their need for social-scientific expertise only as they prepare their dissertations. In addition, the social sciences themselves continue to change rapidly, so that no one can afford to see his diploma as a punctuation mark signaling the end of his education. There is, in short, a clear need for postdoctoral training. Among the historians who answered our questionnaire, by far the greatest demand for summer institutes and years of supplementary training came from those who are only a few years out of graduate school. When they came to proposing specific programs, those same historians suggested postdoctoral fellowships, expanded opportunities for a year at institutions like the Center for Advanced Study in the Behavioral Sciences, and courses in fields like computing, political science, or sociology more often than any other reforms. Although we did not ask the question in just this way, the responses indicate that historians tend to develop the clearest sense of their needs and deficiencies during that time just after the doctorate when they are preparing the materials of their dissertations for publication.

Under present arrangements, few of them can do anything about their desire for further training. We have already seen that these are the years of heaviest teaching load and greatest responsibility for courses outside the young historian's particular interests. Only a few universities finance leave for further education during these years, and only a trivial number of fellowships are available for that purpose. One exception is the small but influential program of research training fellowships of the Social Science Research Council. An increasing proportion of applications to the council have been for postdoctoral support, and an increasing portion of its awards have been for this purpose.

The problem is different for older scholars. Here one of the serious obstacles is the scarcity of full-salary stipends, so that the acceptance of a fellowship usually entails a substantial pecuniary sacrifice. It may well be argued that this is a good thing, in that it selects out those who are most serious and dedicated. Yet the objective here is presumably not so much to promote a higher morality of abnegation, but to facilitate and stimulate significant research. To that end, it is imperative that ways be found to encourage older men to interrupt the routine of their careers and take the time needed to acquire new skills and perceptions. The frequency of such intervals, it should be noted, is a function of the rapidity of intellectual change in the disciplines concerned. In engineering, it is a commonplace that a scholar who has not kept up with the work on the frontiers of the field is no longer competent to teach graduate students after ten years, undergraduates after twenty. In the natural sciences proper, the interval is surely shorter, and the same is more or less true for social-scientific history.

The most important single ingredient is time. The complaints in our questionnaire make this point repeatedly. The faculty member who is burdened with a host of administrative responsibilities, outside commitments to the profession, and sundry other obligations, is compelled to take the easy way out and do his scholarly work in those conventional ways that take the least time and effort. What is more, there is evidence that these supplementary commitments are increasing, especially in these days of campus turmoil.

One thing is clear: the cliché of the conflict between teaching and research is more myth than reality—a kind of scapegoat for the increasing inability of the profession to sustain its manifold obligations in the face of an ever-growing and more demanding clientele. As any good historian knows, the best teachers are those whose own active research keeps them abreast of the latest developments in the field and the opportunities for inquiry; while the best researchers derive inestimable benefit from their contact with students and their obligation to translate difficult, abstruse subject matter into concepts and language intelligible to those less experienced. To be sure, there is in history—though to a much smaller degree than in other disciplines—the academic entrepreneur: the man who spends so much of his time planning and administering research programs that he has no time either for his students or his own work. Yet the presence of such "projectors" is not an argument against research as such. On the contrary *it is precisely the inadequacy of research support that produces such specialists.* If time and money were available to scholars for research as a legitimate and normal concomitant of teaching, there would be far less diversion of effort into the conception of projects with foundation appeal and the preparation of winning applications.

The timing and setting of postdoctoral training should remain flexible. Some historians want an opportunity to move temporarily to another institution to take advantage of work of a particular expert or to benefit from the climate of a setting where specialized work is being conducted. In these cases financed leaves of absence are required. For others, who can find what they need at their own institutions, administrative and teaching obligations should be reduced so as to permit training as a normal feature of academic life. One possibility would be to generalize the institution, already found in some places, of providing beginning teachers a year free from other responsibilities—perhaps the third year of their first contract—for the express purpose of interdisciplinary training. It should be noted realistically, however, that the pressure on young instructors or assistant professors to publish as much as possible with a view to promotion to tenure is so great that many if not most would prefer to use this year to write rather than to learn. This implies that a way must be found to formalize postdoctoral interdisciplinary training, so that the commitment to it is more than just a well-intentioned desire to read the right things. Courses and seminars might be set up for the purpose, comparable to the already familiar summer training institutes, and released time from teaching, over and above such leave time as is already written into the contract, might serve as an additional incentive. The important thing to note is that the present system of promotion puts enormous pressure on the young teacher to get as much written work out as possible and thus encourages him to content himself with the ideas and procedures already learned in graduate school. That so many of these beginning teachers want further training in the social sciences, therefore, is testimony to their intellectual curiosity. It would be a mistake, however, to rely on this alone and not take into account, in promoting this development, the constraints of the system.

Even with this kind of training, however, the historian would not necessarily be in a position to utilize effectively the techniques and concepts of social science in areas outside of those he has been trained in. Ordinarily, such limitations are overcome by personal and intellectual contact with competent colleagues; this is a matter of course in social science departments. Yet given the departmental organization of the university, most historians are cut off from this process of intellectual diffusion unless the nature of their interest brings them together with the kind of interdisciplinary group found in, say, area centers.

More personal contacts between history and social science departments are needed to facilitate this diffusion. One obvious possibility would be to multiply the still uncommon practice of joint appointments. These pose difficult problems for the appointee, who often finds himself trying to satisfy two sets of colleagues by carrying a double load of administrative and departmental obligations. In too many cases, moreover, the appointment is nominal, and the scholar gravitates to one or the other side. In the right circumstances, however, when for example the appointment is linked to a cross-listed course or courses that pull in students and faculty from both sides, these hybrid scholars have been able to play a seminal role with colleagues and students.[1]

Another possibility would be to attach to the history departments specialists in tool disciplines like statistics or computer methods who could then serve as consultants on demand. Admittedly, it would be difficult to persuade senior personnel to accept such an appointment, and even younger specialists might not find enough business to occupy them in any but the largest departments. An alternative would be the establishment, as at the University of North Carolina, of statistical and computing centers to serve more than one depart-

[1] Astonishingly enough, this obvious utilization of cross-listed courses to promote interdisciplinary training is far from a matter of course in many universities, even where the departments concerned are favorable. The passionate determination of registrars and similar bureaucrats to limit "proliferation" and "duplication" (though cross-listing has the effect of preventing duplication), plus a desire to simplify their own task and that of the IBM machines, has produced a ban on cross-listing at a number of universities, for example, the University of California at Berkeley.

ment—perhaps all the behavioral and social sciences including history. The important thing here is not so much the form, which can be adjusted to the needs and possibilities of the institution, but the function: the availability of specialized personnel who are familiar with the special problems of social-scientific history and furnish assistance not as a favor, but as a matter of course.

In support of such arrangements, one may note that the role of consultant-advisor can be and should be far more than one of simple service and accommodation. It would be that, of course: there are historians who would need help with anything more complicated than an arithmetic mean. On the other hand, the limitations of historical evidence and the complexity of the subject matter are such as to make the application of quantitative techniques or social science concepts far more complicated and less routine than in the social sciences themselves. These "translators" can and should, therefore, innovate as well as communicate. Among the most urgent needs, for example, is the development of teaching aids specifically adapted to history. Very few written materials now exist that bring together the ideas and techniques required in useful form. The first text of statistics for the historian is only now being written; hopefully it will play much the same pioneering role as did V. O. Key's *A Primer of Statistics for Political Scientists* fifteen years ago. Even more urgently needed is reading material that takes concepts useful in the social sciences, such as migration and acculturation, economic development, vertical mobility, professionalization, urbanization, bureaucratization, and develops them with the assistance of historical material for a clientele of historians. Some of this material already exists in unpublished form for use in those relatively few courses now given in historical sociology and it could presumably be worked up for a larger public.

It is this pattern that has required historians to pursue their research with only a fraction of the support provided in other disciplines. The Behavioral and Social Sciences Survey Committee's study of social science departments reveals that during the fiscal year 1967 the social sciences (omitting psychology and educational psychology) spent only 45 percent more per student enrolled than did history; but their expenditures for research exceeded those of history by 508 percent.[2]

These data, to be sure, do not include library costs, of which his-

[2] If one includes psychology and educational psychology, the figures are 43 percent more per student and 686 percent more for research.

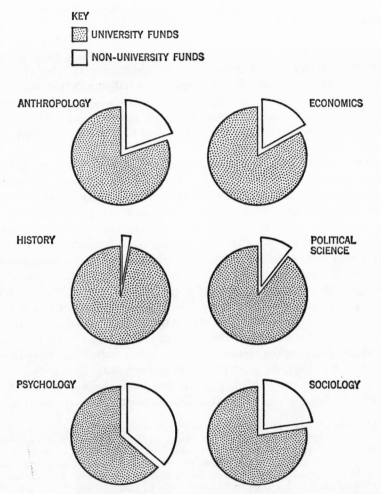

KEY

▨ UNIVERSITY FUNDS

☐ NON-UNIVERSITY FUNDS

ANTHROPOLOGY

ECONOMICS

HISTORY

POLITICAL
SCIENCE

PSYCHOLOGY

SOCIOLOGY

**FIGURE 5-1 TOTAL FUNDS AVAILABLE PER PHD GRANTED,
1967**

From *The Behavioral and Social Sciences: Outlook and Needs*
(Englewood Cliffs, N. J.: Prentice-Hall, Inc., 1969), Tables 9-5,
10-1; pp. 144, 156. The area of the circle is proportionate to the
funds per head; 1 sq. in. equals $15,000 per capita. The funds in
question include all departmental expenditures, not just those for
faculty or graduate students. Consequently, the graph exaggerates
the resources actually available to the average faculty member or
PhD candidate in fields, like political science and history, with
large undergraduate enrollments.

tory accounts for a substantial share. It would be desirable for the purposes of this discussion to allocate library expenditures by department, but the statistics are not available. Besides, even if they were, it would obviously be incorrect to assume that acquisitions for one discipline were not of interest and value to another. In a sense, libraries are the general property of the community of scholars, and no one can predict at any given time who will find what useful in the future. In the meantime, the committee's survey does reveal that other social science departments are almost twice as likely to have departmental libraries as history, and that when they do, their library budgets are half again as large.[3]

This gap between history and the social sciences derives partly from the nature of the work. No matter how rapid the course of technological innovation, much historical research will always consist of slow, often painstaking and tedious reading and analysis of literary texts. There is no place for costly experiments, and the kind of quantitative analysis that calls for expensive hardware will always constitute only one sector of the discipline. Yet it is a sector that is growing in importance, and the discipline as a whole has been won over by some forms of technological progress—in particular, by those new photographic and copying devices that have transformed the central act of note-taking. At the same time, social-scientific historians have been learning more about what can be done to facilitate their work by observing the facilities accorded other disciplines. They have been mixing with the rich and learning new wants. This demonstration effect will, one hopes, generate the kind of demand that will diffuse within the profession and elicit an adequate response.

[3] Seventy-five percent higher if psychology is omitted. Admittedly many historians feel that they are adequately served by large general collections, and some would even argue that departmental libraries constitute a diversion of resources. With all due allowance, however, for the dangers posed by an excessive dispersion of specialized materials, we feel that this point of view underestimates the contribution that a departmental collection of standard reference works and monographs can make to communication within the field. It also reflects the low expectations of the discipline in regard to convenience. None of the natural sciences would put up with isolation from those books that have to be consulted frequently, and in some disciplines—chemistry, for example—the department cannot even be accredited if its laboratories and the relevant library collections are not found within the same building.

SUPPORT FOR AND ORGANIZATION
OF RESEARCH

Traditionally historical research has been carried on by the individual historian working directly with materials that he himself has collected. He utilizes no equipment and only occasionally has research assistance. His expenses are confined to his own living costs. He usually schedules his research for those times when he is on leave from teaching duties, sometimes on a sabbatical leave, sometimes on research grants from the few agencies that provide them, and at times on a combination of the two. He rarely collaborates with others, whether graduate students or faculty colleagues. All this entails no involvement of larger groups or organizations, within or without the scholar's own institution.

What do historians need?

Personnel and Equipment

First, they need more secretarial assistance. This is routine in the natural sciences and the social sciences, if only because it would be impermissible in these areas to expect highly paid teachers and scholars to spend a substantial fraction of their time writing letters, typing manuscripts and reports, and taking notes. The relative scarcity of such assistance in fields like history and, even more, the humanities, constitutes in effect a judgment about the marginal utility of time for their members. To be sure, universities tend to be impartial in their parsimony in this regard. It is the extra-university sources that make the difference: in 1967, for example, such sources provided twenty times as much support for this purpose to social science departments as to history. Especially needed is a job category best described as "research secretary" that would combine the conventional typing and shorthand skills with ancillary research skills: a knowledge of foreign languages and scripts, familiarity with statistics and statistical presentation, an ability to handle bibliographical materials.

In addition, new modes of research—and old—require the support of a whole range of specialists, from map and chart makers, to reference librarians and iconographers, to materials scientists, to statisticians and programmers. In this respect, history has been disadvantaged both within and without the university, as Table 4-1 shows. In 1967, other social science departments (omitting psychology and educational psychology) received from their universities three times as much for this purpose as history; while extra-university sources provided them with eighteen times as much support. Similarly, the other social sciences (again omitting psychology) received well over twice as much from the university for graduate research assistants and eight and a half times as much from outside sources.[4]

The gap is even wider in regard to equipment. In fiscal 1967, the mean permanent equipment purchases for the social sciences (omitting psychology) was three and a half times that for history, while the disparity of outside funding was of the order of seventeen to one.[5] Again, some difference is to be expected, but the difference is clearly too large, in the sense that historians find it difficult to gain access to and utilize the equipment they do need: individual microfilm readers, calculators, microprint facilities, microfilm cameras. To be sure, many if not all of these facilities are usually available through central photographic and microfilm divisions in libraries. Yet this merely shifts the problem. The question that then arises is the extent of support for these services: does the historian have the money to use them as required? For most the answer is no.

The problem is especially acute in field research. Here the work of the scholar has been transformed by the copying revolution, which has drastically altered the ratios of time spent reading to time spent note-taking. Whereas an old-fashioned researcher relying on pen or pencil will usually give three hours or more to writing for every hour spent reading (this will obviously vary with the density of the reading matter) the proportion has now been reversed by the increased availability of microfilm and copying facilities, even in secondary libraries or poorer countries. The constraints here are usually two: In many places, service is extremely slow and otherwise unsatisfactory, and there is some advantage in being able to use one's own photographic equipment. Second, this kind of work can be extremely expensive, and only those who have been fortunate enough to receive funds earmarked for the purpose are in a position to pay the fees.

[4] If one includes psychology and educational psychology, the respective proportions are twenty-six to one for research support personnel and thirteen to one for graduate research assistants.

[5] If one includes psychology and educational psychology, the respective proportions are ten to one for all equipment purchases and ninety-three to one for outside funding.

Even so, most researchers—including impecunious graduate students —have found it advantageous to pay for copying even at personal expense, if only because of the high overhead cost of work away from home. All of these considerations, obviously, are also relevant at home, though in lesser degree.

The computer poses special difficulties. Most institutions have data-processing equipment sufficient technically for the needs of historians, but the equipment is underused by historians. While the average history department used 5 hours of computer time in 1967, the average social science department used 146 hours. In the meantime, the volume of material that lends itself to machine analysis and manipulation is growing rapidly, altering the composition of the corpus of historical evidence. The historian will inevitably use the computer more as time goes on, and with it such accessory devices as sorters and remote-control consoles. At the moment, however, the major weakness is the lack of software. Historians who use computers have special requirements, very different from those of other users; much of what they do, for example, entails rather simple manipulation of masses of data, rather than the more customary complex manipulation of limited data, so that inputs are high in relation to output. At the same time, because the historian knows little about computer procedures he is especially dependent on the services of programmers and other technicians.

The Organization of Research

In general, the progress of social-scientific historical research is impeded by the inefficient use of time and talent; and this is not simply a matter of equipment. One of the most serious difficulties is the inadequacy of the communications—both between faculty and students and within the faculty.

Nothing is more indicative of this than the persistent separation between research and teaching. We have already noted the tendency to look at these as mutually exclusive and competitive—to the point where the alleged absenteeism of teachers has become one of the hottest issues of the student revolt. The problem, as we have seen, lies in large part with the traditional organization of courses, which creates a profound division between the teacher's creative world, his world of excitement and inspiration, and his "job world"; and the situation is aggravated by the physical separation of research and teaching. This is why we feel it is so important to revive the seminar-workshop as it was originally conceived in Germany and once existed in this country. Such an arrangement is the direct analogue of the teaching laboratory in the natural sciences, but the scientists have had the good sense to maintain it, while historians have abandoned it.

The divorce between research and teaching is reinforced by the general reluctance of history teachers to steer their doctoral students into those avenues of inquiry that they (the teachers) look upon as fruitful and by the tendency of students to look upon this kind of direction as a form of exploitation. The general feeling that prevails is "every man for himself" and the corollary assumption is that anything that smacks of an assignment of topic is an effort to turn the graduate student from independent scholar into glorified research assistant. There is some truth in this, and natural scientists are the first to deplore the abuses of the assignment arrangements that prevail in their fields.[6] Even so, the optimum arrangement would obviously fall somewhere in between. At present, a great deal of the talent in history is dispersed by the winds of fashion and whimsey, with the result that the frontiers of the discipline move forward sporadically and haphazardly. Much work is devoted to isolated and trivial subjects that are unfortunately not trivial to the people working on them, and the consequent output of verbiage is often cited as the strongest argument against the institution of the doctoral dissertation. Even those who see the dissertation as a valuable feature of graduate training—and they are a substantial majority of graduate history faculties—feel that the typical thesis is too long and too ambitious and a substantial fraction would like to see the dissertation reduced in scope to a training exercise.[7]

Yet there is nothing wrong with the doctoral dissertation that a better distribution of scholarly effort couldn't cure. On the contrary, the evidence is that for many historians, the doctoral thesis is the one substantial piece of work they will do in their entire lifetime, which is all the more reason to make the effort worthwhile and to turn more of these years of labor and pounds of notes into signifi-

[6] For some complaints on this score, see National Academy of Sciences, *The Invisible University: Postdoctoral Education in the United States* (Washington, D. C., 1969), pp. 184–85. Most scientists, however, are careful to distinguish abuses from the norm and strongly endorse the principle of related, interlocking research in the laboratory context.

[7] According to the Perkins-Snell report, about one out of three historians feels this way. Our impression is that, if anything, the proportion has risen since then. Perkins and Snell, *The Education of Historians*, p. 151.

cant contributions. To be sure, there is no reason why a well-trained graduate student cannot choose topics of inquiry that are likely to produce such results. Indeed, the most important thing to be learned about research is how to select an intellectually important problem. Yet there will always be some students who need and can profit from closer guidance, at least the first time, especially within the context of interrelated, mutually supportive research.

It is within this context also that what is now a somewhat deprecated institution in the field of history, the role of research professor, can find its justification. The different attitudes of history on the one hand and the natural and social sciences on the other to such appointments are striking testimony to the way in which the present divorce of research and teaching distorts the possibilities of the historical profession. The natural and social scientists look upon appointments to research professorships as a legitimate use of funds to attract those scholars who are working on the frontiers of the discipline and should be released from the ordinary duties of instruction to pursue their own inquiries and to serve as a model and inspiration to advanced students. The historical profession, by contrast, tends to look upon this august status—not without empirical justification—as a privileged form of premature retirement from legitimate teaching obligations. Understandably, there is some hostility to an arrangement that is viewed as inequitable and potentially subversive of that commitment to teaching that is rightly seen as one of the strengths of the profession. Yet if the proper institutional arrangements could be found to combine these privileges with new opportunities for instruction on an advanced level—precisely the kind of thing that would be possible in a workshop seminar—much of this hostility would in time disappear.

A more effective organization of research calls for more collaboration and contact among faculty as well as between faculty and students. Joint research is common in the natural and social sciences; it is strange to the historian, who has customarily worked alone. Yet the task of social-scientific history often requires more expertise than one researcher can provide, so that to confine one's research to what can be managed by one man is to render the product limited, parochial, and substantially less useful than it might be. To make the most of potentially fruitful comparisons and of the concepts and procedures of other social sciences often requires the expansion of research design to combine the efforts of more than one scholar. Yet the profession frowns on this—again perhaps, on

the basis of empirical experience. It is not easy for two or more
people to join in the writing of anything. Such groups are usually
no stronger than their weakest member. On the other hand, there
is no reason why such groups would have to collaborate in the production of a single, joint work. More often than not, they will find
it more efficient and congenial to allow each member to prepare his
own study, so that collaboration takes the form of communication
and mutual support. The important thing is to promote that proximity of endeavor that makes possible this support, and research
resources should be distributed accordingly.

Collaboration takes many forms. One of the most successful is
periodic or ad hoc meetings of scholars with similar interests to
discuss a common problem; the proliferation of these colloquia in
recent years, sometimes at the personal expense of the participants,
is testimony to their usefulness. Specialists in Japanese studies from
many different disciplines, for example, have been holding a regular
series of meetings since 1966 dealing with the development of research in the field and with specific problems like the modernization
of Japan. Some of these groups have been financed by foundations;
the Social Science Research Council has been particularly active in
this area. Others have depended on university support; the "University Seminars" of Columbia University represent the prototype:
beginning with scholars from the New York City area, they have
expanded to include a wide interdisciplinary range and to bring in
participants from Maine to Virginia. Sometimes, however, these
groups have been a spontaneous expression of the need to exchange
ideas and criticism: economic historians have been meeting for some
years now in the San Francisco area (Berkeley and Stanford) and
in the Boston area (Harvard and M.I.T.) once a month to talk
about the field and discuss one another's papers. In a world of polite
book reviews and heavy commitments, this kind of mutual stimulation and criticism is hard to come by. The proof of the value of
such meetings is the record of attendance.

Money cannot buy this kind of thing. All it can do is to facilitate
collaboration and contact where the scholars themselves recognize
their desirability. Money can, however, stimulate those forms of
cooperation that exceed the possibilities of the private person:
regional or international meetings, for example, that bring people
together from some distance; or meetings of some duration requiring
residential facilities for the participants. Here the universities, with
their tremendous competition for limited space, are often less well

equipped to do the job than are independent institutes and libraries; and it is no coincidence that more and more such sessions have been held at places like the Newberry Library in Chicago, the Huntington Library in Los Angeles, or the Eleutherian Mills Historical Library near Wilmington. Such centers, plus such new ones as might develop as a consequence of library expansion, should be encouraged and assisted to pursue this line of activity further. It is not only that they are in many ways better placed to accommodate such meetings; even more important, it is often an advantage to participants to get away from their home institutions and to be able to give their full attention to the business at hand. Not only are they spared the incessant disruption of teaching and administrative obligations, but they are also wrenched out of what is often a fixed and inflexible pattern of relationships and freed to make the most of new personal and intellectual contacts.

This liberation effect is most strikingly observed in those centers that transport the scholar entirely out of his normal frame of reference into a new world by means of fellowships of some duration. Here too, some libraries have found the means to play a modest role, but the most prominent examples of this kind of support are the major interdisciplinary research centers like The Institute for Advanced Study in Princeton and the Center for Advanced Study in the Behavioral Sciences in Stanford. It is a sad but significant commentary on the nature of the university that scholars transferred to these settings find it much easier to know and work with persons interested in similar problems, even persons from their own home institution. The departmental boundaries, the heavy demands of courses and students, the complicated and time-consuming pattern of personal and social obligations at home—all combine to make it extremely difficult to make the most of the intellectual possibilities of a university community; and it is precisely the liberation from all these constraints that is the greatest contribution of the independent research center. Again, the natural sciences seem to suffer from these handicaps far less than other disciplines—unquestionably in large part owing to the functional contribution of the laboratory as a vehicle for both teaching and research.

It is in this context that one can best evaluate the potential contribution of the projected Woodrow Wilson International Center for Scholars in Washington, D. C. (signed into law October 25, 1968). The plans for this center are not yet fixed, and there is still some question whether it should receive only temporary members,

like the Center for Advanced Study in the Behavioral Sciences, or
have a permanent research staff of its own, like the Institute for
Advanced Study. We would opt for the latter, not only because
the nation's capital has long needed a more substantial resident
faculty of scholars in the social sciences to match the comparable
faculties assembled at such places as the National Institute for
Mental Health, but also because such a group would provide a focus
for continuing research and make possible the cumulation of results over a period of years. As for visitors, they should range from
advanced graduate students to senior scholars and include foreigners
as well as Americans. Given the extraordinary resources and at-
tractions of the Washington area to students of the behavioral and
social sciences, the absence of this kind of center has been a flagrant
example of missed opportunities. If the Woodrow Wilson Center
turns out to be as productive as its circumstances would seem to
warrant, it may well in turn serve as a model for similar centers in
other parts of the country.

As the above discussion makes clear, history has long been disadvantaged in facilities and support for research. This is most keenly
felt at the level of the individual scholar, who finds that he has few
places to turn to for the kind of help that other disciplines have
come to look upon as normal and indispensable. The situation can
best be understood in terms of the opportunity available to the
individual scholar working, say, on the history of child rearing in
the nineteenth century. Under certain narrowly specified conditions,
such a person could apply to the Social Science Research Council;
he could also turn to the Guggenheim Foundation or other granting
agencies of a general character, though the resources of these institutions are too limited to admit of full stipends. The National
Endowment for the Humanities is similarly limited: its primary
commitment is to letters, languages, and philosophy, and to that
humanistic side of history which is even less well provided for than
the social-scientific sector. Given the breadth of its coverage, it is
hardly surprising that the forty to fifty grants not exceeding $10,000
proposed in 1968–69 were far from realizing the high hopes that had
been placed in this institution, the more so as support was concentrated on projects "whose results might have direct implications for
present and emerging national problems."

One could continue this list *diminuendo*, ranging from the "richer"
agencies to the lesser. The point is simply that the historian, even
the social-scientific historian, faces extremely severe competition for

the few grants available in his field and has learned in most instances to content himself with little or nothing. In particular, he is substantially cut off from the largest single funding agency, the National Science Foundation, which, as we have seen, incorporated in its directives a prohibition of grants to historians, even those working on subjects substantially identical with those financed under other rubrics.

The only way in which historians have managed to get around these difficulties is to shelter under the umbrella of an interdisciplinary program or institute. Thus the Joint Center for Urban Studies of M.I.T.-Harvard, the Institute of Industrial Relations of the University of California, Berkeley, and a whole range of area centers throughout the country have always reserved some of their resources for historical research. Clearly, however, not all social-scientific historians are doing work that falls within the purview of one of these organizations or are teaching in places where such potential funding agencies are to be found. For these people, new sources of support must be created, on the national, regional, or local level.

It would be presumptuous to pretend that any such program of general funding for individual and group historical research will yield a harvest of new knowledge in specified areas. There is no doubt that more generous support would generate new and more useful knowledge in a wide variety of domains: social structure and change, population patterns, modernization, race relations, urbanization, ecological pressures and responses. History, in spite of stereotypes, is extremely sensitive to contemporary concerns, and would be quick to respond to opportunities for research along these lines; but it is not in the nature of the subject to be able to produce results on order, as is possible in some fields of science and engineering, where one can with some probability promise solutions to given problems within an approximate period in return for a given outlay of time and effort.

What increased financing could be expected to produce is a new pattern of activity. The historian who now finds it necessary to write or to promise textbooks and other teaching aids, to an extent that far exceeds the needs of the discipline and serves only the competition of commercial publishers, would then be in a position to devote more of his time to the kind of scholarship that often drew him into the field in the first place. At the same time both teachers and students would no longer have to truncate or alter their subjects to take into account constraints of time and money. These con-

straints have been especially inhibiting to those who would undertake the kind of comparative inquiry that entails field research,
especially field research abroad; so that it would not be unreasonable
to expect a far healthier balance of effort in the American historical
unity between those projects that are defined by convenience (which
often means topics bounded by one or two shelves in the library)
and those topics that start from a problem and embrace all the
relevant sources, wherever they may be.

What this means, in other words, is that while it is impossible to
promise results or answers in a field like history, it is reasonable to
expect a substantial shift in the direction and character of historical
inquiry in response to a program of support comparable to that
available in other social sciences. Lest there be any misunderstanding,
moreover, this is the kind of shift that would affect all sectors of
historical inquiry, not only social-scientific history. The entire field
is presently hampered and impoverished by inadequate support, so
that scholars in all branches tend to retreat to the source-determined
subject, rather than venture into the problem-oriented inquiry; and
to fall back on the convenience of conventional time-and-space
courses. The historian has in essence created and fallen victim to a
culture of poverty: by comparison with colleagues in other disciplines, he is poor and either does not know it, does not care, or
makes a virtue of it. Money will not give him virtues he does not
possess; but it will make it possible for him to realize his under-
realized potential.

In consideration of these needs and circumstances, we would like
to offer the following recommendations:

1. That both public and private granting agencies expand the
range and level of support for historical research. Specifically, the
National Science Foundation should not only redefine social science
so as to include social-scientific history but commit itself to an
active program for its encouragement. To this end, it should appoint
representatives of history to its administrative and governing bodies.
To the extent that the National Science Foundation is uninterested
in such a program or sees it as either foreign to its mission or of
lesser significance or priority than its present areas of concern, we
would strongly urge the establishment of the proposed National
Social Science Foundation, with a clear mandate to support the full
range of historical research.

2. That departments of history build into their budgets and treat

as normal costs of operation the salaries of technical secretaries and research assistants, charges for computer time and photographic and photocopy work for both faculty and students, and the cost of such equipment (microfilm readers, calculators, dictating machines, and so forth) as faculty and staff require for their individual research.

3. That universities, in collaboration with public and private funding agencies, make available to historians more flexible leave and travel arrangements, so that it will be possible on the one hand, to work in the field or at another institution for more than the conventional year, and on the other hand, to make shorter trips of two to six weeks. The former arrangement would presumably be rare, if only because of the inconvenience to most scholars of so long an interruption of their residence, the normal schooling of their children, and their own teaching responsibilities. There will, however, be instances where such a prolonged stay is advisable—for example, where research is combined with and dependent on a program of retraining, or where participation in a group research project entails prolonged continuous collaboration. In such cases, the biggest obstacle is liable to be the unwillingness of the home university to release its faculty for so long a period—for obvious, cogent reasons. Yet there is a clear need for some loosening of these constraints, perhaps in conjunction with greater mobility for graduate students as proposed in the previous chapter. This would ease somewhat the demands for resident supervision of dissertations and, in combination with a program of postdoctoral-cum-teaching-fellowships, would make possible a richer experience for the apprentice scholar. (There are some who will say that this kind of flexibility is utopian, but in years to come, universities are going to be making any number of adjustments of this kind to accommodate the special needs and responsibilities of women scholars. What they can do for women, they can do for all.)

Shorter trips are much less a threat to conventional teaching arrangements, but much more difficult to finance. The usual fellowships and stipends make no provision for this kind of quick probe, and yet the transformation of the technology of research has made short sojourns far more productive than before. They are particularly useful as sequels to earlier, longer trips, enabling the scholar to fill in gaps in, or to verify particular aspects of, his research; or, conversely, they can in difficult cases prepare the ground and insure that a longer visit will not be half lost for want of contacts or experience.

4. That public and private funding agencies finance a program of postdoctoral fellowships of two or three years for those historians who would like to obtain further interdisciplinary training before entering on a full-time teaching appointment. Such fellows would presumably combine this with research and writing—perhaps the revision of the dissertation for publication, perhaps some new project; and some would no doubt undertake light teaching responsibilities, perhaps in the context of a workshop seminar. This is a common pattern in the natural sciences, where such arrangements have generally been highly productive, both to the fellow and his host institution. They have been far less common in the social sciences and humanities, partly for financial reasons, partly (it is argued) for reasons of timing: the postdoctoral years are not the most creative in disciplines where intellectual power depends considerably on the accumulation of knowledge and on maturity of judgment.[8] On the other hand, if such fellowships constituted an opportunity to learn as well as to do research, they would be ideally suited to a field like history, where existing programs of graduate study leave little time for interdisciplinary training.

5. That colleges and universities in collaboration with public and private funding agencies, finance the establishment and operations of interuniversity colloquia, seminars, and workshops on an ad hoc or continuing basis, where the demand exists and circumstances warrant. In particular, it would be desirable to link in this way stronger and weaker institutions, centrally located schools and isolated ones. Where local history is relevant, local historians, in and out of academia, should be drawn into the program. The workshop-seminars recommended in Chapter 4 above might well serve as the domicile for such local or regional associations; so also could research libraries and more specialized research facilities like the center for work in collective biography now being organized at Princeton or repositories of data archives like Michigan's Inter-University Consortium for Political Research.

[8] National Research Council, *The Invisible University: Postdoctoral Education in the United States* (Washington, D. C.: National Academy of Sciences, 1969), p. 192.

6
FOREIGN RESEARCH

Far more than other social scientists, with the exception of the anthropologists, historians must work abroad. For most of them—indeed, for an increasing majority of them—that is where the evidence is. There was a time when the only serious competitor to the United States for historians' attention was Europe.[1] Now the whole world is their province.

Where there is evidence, there are resident scholars. The quality of work done abroad by native historians varies enormously from one country to another. The best scholarship is to be found in Europe—the homeland, as it were, of "scientific" history. (Some of these developments on the intellectual frontier of the discipline are discussed in Chapter 3 above.) The weakest, sparsest work comes from Third World countries, which are generally busy with other things and, further, often lack the heritage and experience needed to provide the standards and cadres of a historical discipline. Even these are beginning, however, to make a serious contribution to the literature, and one can reasonably anticipate a substantial convergence of quality between old and new centers of scholarship. Where long historical traditions like those of China and India are available, we

[1] It is interesting in this regard to compare the distribution of doctorates by geographical area of specialization and the distribution of appointments. From 1955 through 1959, 51.0 percent of history PhD's were awarded in United States history, 38.4 percent in European, 10.4 percent in all other fields. By way of contrast, anticipated faculty appointments by field in 1958–59 were 35 percent United States, 37 percent European (including eastern Europe), and 28 percent other. The students, in other words, had not yet moved in this direction, but this was where history departments were going. Perkins and Snell, *The Education of Historians*, pp. 31–32.

might expect eventually to see historical work of unmatched richness and continuity.

As a result, a larger portion of significant original work is done outside the United States in history than in the other social sciences. Even where the foreign scholar is no more than a collector and transcriber of data, he has the advantage of proximity to the sources; and as any American working on the history of a foreign country can testify, this makes possible a richness of documentation and a thoroughness of coverage that even the greatest diligence and efficiency cannot match. In a profession that places a high value on erudition, this is an important advantage. (David Pinkney once argued that for this reason American scholars have not been and never will be able to compete with French researchers in their contributions to French history.)

In many instances, however, this "home team" advantage is more than compensated for by the visitor's outside perspective, especially one that lays stress on international comparisons and is combined with an interdisciplinary approach. There are European scholars who feel that American historians, with their more broadly defined topics and more speculative social-scientific interpretations, are superficial poachers creaming off the most exciting material and sacrificing nuance and depth to facile, attention-getting generalizations. Some of this censure is justified; some of it comes from pique and insecurity. Whatever its psychological components, it is a response to what has up to now been a kind of division of labor that many foreign scholars want to get away from.[2]

The problem is even more acute in those countries where historical research is still in its infancy—the academically underdeveloped countries. Here the disparity between American and indigenous researchers is far greater. We come with our IBM cards and computer tapes to places where scholars still work with pencil and notebook. We have funds for photography and photocopying, sometimes even our own cameras and portable copying machines, whereas they must still take everything down by hand. We are familiar—at least some

[2] They are in fact getting away from it. Foreign scholars are less and less parochial. Like American historians, they are beginning to be interested in other countries as well as their own; they are also becoming increasingly familiar with social science concepts and techniques. On the other hand, thanks to more efficient research methods, American scholars are now able to accomplish far more work in the relatively short stays they can make in foreign centers, with consequent improvement in their documentation. Here too, then, is a process of convergence.

of us are—with computer techniques and are ready to convert our quantitative data to machine-readable form, whereas they are still adding and multiplying by hand. The disparity can be important even by comparison with a technologically advanced country like France. At a meeting in 1968 at the Institute for Social Research of the University of Michigan held to discuss the possibility of an international program for the storage of official statistical records in a computer data bank, the French representatives argued for restricted access to the material. When it was pointed out to them that this was all printed material in the public domain, their reply was that their students were not prepared as yet to make the most of the opportunities presented by the conversion of the data to machine-readable form and that under the circumstances, foreign scholars (read: American scholars) would harvest the first and richest fruits of this endeavor. This was France, which is more sensitive than most countries to foreign "competition" in the intellectual sphere and more proprietary than most about its history. Yet one finds even greater sensitivity in the nations of the Third World, where foreign scholarship is linked or assimilated, if only in the perception of international relations, to acts of political or economic imperialism. In Turkey, no archival document may be shown to a foreign scholar until it has been seen and used (or released) by Turkish historians. And in Thailand, no visiting anthropologist is supposed to remove his notes from the country until he has filed a preliminary report of his findings.

The implementation of the research program recommended in Chapter 5 would certainly, in the short run, increase the disparity between the resources of American scholars abroad and those of indigenous scholars. We are asking for more funds for foreign research, as well as domestic, a more flexible leave policy, and the extensive use of those photographic and electronic devices that multiply the productivity of the scholar. More than ever, the American historian abroad, like the American political scientist or anthropologist, is going to look in some countries like a human cargo ship, bringing the fruits of modern technology to backward peoples.

It goes without saying that the existence of this problem is not an argument for curtailing field work abroad. This would be a kind of intellectual isolationism and would only impoverish American historical research as well as that of other countries. The aim is not to cut us off from one another but to promote communication, contact, and possible collaboration, and to do this in such a way as to enrich both sides. (In a way, it is unfortunate that considerations of this kind should ever have raised their ugly heads; but these are the facts of scholarly life, and we must face up to them, if only because the results are substantially better if one is sensitive to them.)

What can be done to promote the right kind of communication and contact? The first thing is to develop a better balance of intellectual payments. We should begin to see the movement of American researchers abroad as part of a two-way flow and to assist foreign historians to come to the United States as researchers and teachers. Up to now, the high cost of living in the United States and foreign exchange difficulties have discouraged many from coming, even from accepting visiting appointments; and such appointments as have been effected have more often than not been desultory, a haphazard response to a temporary vacancy in the teaching staff. What is needed is a more regular flow of visitors, short and long, selected with some regard to the systematic enrichment of the program of instruction and research. Obviously not all visitors would satisfy this criterion, nor should they. But all departments of history would be significantly strengthened if they could rely, as a matter of course, on the collaboration of a stream of foreign scholars, so chosen as to fill gaps in the regular offerings.

Such an arrangement, in our opinion, affords important advantages over the "grand tours" currently sponsored by the federal government and a number of philanthropic foundations. These tours, which take the visitor to a half-dozen or more places in the space of a few weeks or months, do provide him with a sense of the variety of American society and education. Yet he rarely comes to know any one place well, or those people in it whom he hasn't already met in his own country; nor does he derive from his travels that intellectual benefit that comes from participation in teaching and research; nor do his hosts derive the benefits that this participation could bring them.

To be sure, institutional arrangements in themselves are not enough to insure that people will in fact collaborate, get to know one another, and profit one another. Coming to a place is not equivalent to integration in it, as many an unhappy visitor knows. Still, much could be done to promote such integration by facilitating and regularizing the contacts—by making them normal rather than exceptional. University housing should include, as a matter of course, facilities for guests (including their dependents). Office space should also be set aside for visitors. And departments should be enabled to budget in advance for a continuing flow of outsiders, in such a way that students can count on these additional offerings and plan their own programs accordingly. In some instances, it may be desirable to develop permanent or quasi-permanent pairing arrangements between a department here and one abroad, especially when the teaching staffs and course offerings complement each other. Such pairings are not easy to carry out, since all concerned have obligations at home that impose severe constraints on movement and since the convenience of the group is not always the convenience of its individual members. Moreover these obligations and constraints can only be expected to increase as more and more spouses assume professional commitments of their own. Even so, the answer does not lie in surrender to these constraints, but rather in by-passing them. In a context of more flexible leave arrangements, more generous funding for travel, and a more imaginative organization of courses (such as team teaching or alternating periods of teaching and research), what now seems both inconvenient and utopian may well look reasonable and feasible.

A more even balance of intellectual payments would do much to improve relations within the international scholarly community. For one thing, it would help dissipate the sense, which some national scholarly communities have, of a knowledge drain into the United States. For another, it should (assuming normal hospitality and good will) add substantially to that corps of scholars whose ties to the American intellectual community enable them to play the role of hosts and intermediaries for American scholars in their own countries.

This is extremely important. A study of the *Responsibilities of the Foreign Scholar to the Local Scholarly Community,* published by the Council on Educational Cooperation with Latin America, makes it clear that in many instances, especially in Third World countries, the ties of the visiting American scholar or student to the local scholarly community are crucial to the success of his research. It is desirable, they argue, that the visitor frame his project with some regard to the opinions of local scholars; that he convey to these a sense of his competence (linguistic and otherwise) to carry out the project; that he work insofar as possible with the advice and, if a student, under the benevolent supervision of a local scholar; that he affiliate if possible with local teaching or research institutions; that he contribute, when and if asked, to local scholarly and teaching activities; that he teach his techniques to local researchers; and that

he communicate his findings periodically to the local scholarly community.[3] Along the same lines, the visiting researcher should, whenever possible, send back to the host country a copy of his material,
especially of machine-readable data. That he should also send copies
of his published work goes without saying. It might also be desirable in some instances to arrange for translations of this work into
the language of the host country (assuming that the work is worth
translating), and it would often be extremely useful to provide for
a return trip for the specific purpose of discussing and analyzing
the finished product. Such a second visit might also be the occasion for reviewing with local scholars and students the research
techniques employed.

None of this, obviously, is a sure-fire formula. Since difficulties
and misunderstandings in this area are in part, often in large part,
of psychic origin, recourse to institutionalized courtesies and procedures of mutual assistance will not solve all of the problem. Yet
it is a beginning and, given the fundamental commitment almost
all scholars feel to knowledge and free inquiry, can open the way
to the removal of suspicion and anxiety. Thus the initial impasse
over French-American collaboration in the collection of machine-
readable statistical data was in fact broken as a result of negotiation
and sweet reason. The probability of such happy endings is considerably enhanced by an awareness of the issue.

To promote and facilitate historical research abroad and continuing and fruitful communication with foreign scholars, we offer
the following recommendations:

1. That the federal government and private funding agencies establish, in conjunction with stipends for American scholars working
abroad, counterpart funds to finance research and training visits by
foreign scholars to the United States. These visitors should be attached to one or more scholarly institutions in this country and
integrated so far as possible into the regular research or teaching
programs of such institutions. The timing and duration of such visits
should be sufficiently flexible to meet the requirements of foreign
academic calendars as well as our own.

2. That the exchange implied by the previous recommendation
be regularized when possible and desirable in the form of pairings

---

[3] Richard N. Adams, ed., *Responsibilities of the Foreign Scholar to the Local
Scholarly Community: Studies of U.S. Research in Guatemala, Chile and Para-
guay* (Education and World Affairs, 1969), pp. 8–9.

or groupings of American and foreign institutions for purposes of teaching and joint research. Such arrangements should be sufficiently stable to permit students to plan their training accordingly and should be combined with provisions for student travel and joint degrees.

3. That American scholars working abroad affiliate when possible with foreign academic institutions; that, whenever possible, they provide these host institutions with copies of their data as well as the usual copies of their finished work; and that, where appropriate, they make themselves available to teach their techniques and explain their findings to students and scholars of the host country.

4. That American universities and private funding agencies join in establishing abroad permanent work centers for American scholars engaged in field research. These centers, which would serve the whole range of scholarly disciplines, would provide those facilities that the academic institutions of the host country were not in a position to furnish and accommodate the needs of unaffiliated American scholars and students: desks and office space, recording and photocopy equipment, secretarial help, translation services, even assistance with housing and similar personal concerns. These facilities should not serve as a substitute for affiliation with and work at foreign academic institutions; they should not become enclaves of American scholars clinging to one another in a strange land. But there are any number of reasons why an American scholar would find it helpful to work in such a center for a brief period, or to borrow equipment, or to use its facilities in addition to those provided by a foreign host. The cost of such an establishment would vary with the range of its services and the activity of American scholarship in the area; to some extent, the success of the facility would increase its clientele. Initial outlays, especially for space and installation, would be heavy. Current expenses could be recovered in part from users' fees.

7

LIBRARIES, ARCHIVES, AND OTHER REPOSITORIES

One would have thought that in a report focusing on social-scientific history and historians, we could have left the question of libraries to librarians. Yet a properly equipped library is as crucial to most branches of the social sciences and humanities as the laboratory or observatory is to the natural and physical sciences. For the student of man, the library contains not only the reports of his fellow investigators, but also much of the raw material of his inquiry.

No one depends more on the library than the historian. Since, unlike the sociologist using survey techniques or the psychologist running experiments, the historian cannot create his evidence, he must take his material where he finds it, usually in widely dispersed places. Only occasionally, by setting a problem to fit the sources, can he count on a high density of evidence and a correspondingly high return on effort. More commonly, he must scour the library far and wide, for he never knows when that additional article or monograph will provide the missing piece in his puzzle.

What is more, historical research is not so cumulative as research in chemistry, biology, or even economics. As new approaches develop, new questions are asked, new insights are gained, new interpretations are suggested, and the corpus of historical judgment and knowledge must be reappraised. These reappraisals in turn undergo their own critical review as perspectives lengthen, new questions are posed, and new generations appear. To answer these questions, historians must not only reread the books, articles, and primary sources of their teachers, but inevitably, must turn to sources unused by their predecessors. Hence it is impossible at any point in time to know what is going to be important. Potentially, almost anything that is written is important, and it is the task of a good library to act as the repository not only of those materials needed today but of those that will be needed tomorrow. To the written record, moreover, the modern historian would add taped materials, photographs, films, models, artifacts, and other iconographic evidence.

In this connection, the rapid increase in the level of communications in recent years has created special and severe problems for the preservation of evidence for future historical research. The increased use of the telephone for messages about which no record is kept imposes a special and unsolvable limitation. Even so, there is more material than we can handle, and the cost of storage is so high that it is hard to resist the impulse to save money by destroying noncurrent information. In other words, if the historian waits several decades before he becomes concerned about the availability of evidence for his research, it will be far too late; the record will already have vanished. It is imperative, therefore, that we have agencies which can play the role intermediate between the record-creator and the record-user, which will approach problems of preservation seriously with the future needs of the historian in mind, and which will take the lead in developing wise record-management programs appropriate to future research.

Considerable attention and support, therefore, are needed to meet the growing and changing demands placed on a scholarly library. This is not a luxury; it is indispensable. The Cartter Report, which assessed the relative prestige of different departments in American graduate education, demonstrates the close connection between estimates of the quality of research and quality of library holdings. In a few cases (chiefly because of extraordinary laboratory facilities), institutions with poor library resources have achieved strength in some fields. They are exceptions, however, and are only found in the areas of natural science and engineering. Omitting the 3 leading institutions of science and technology, the 17 leading universities had library holdings ranging from 1.3 million to nearly 9 million volumes, with an average of 2.7 million. The lowest 20 among 106 institutions studied had libraries ranging from 125,000 to a million volumes, averaging 450,000.[1]

These libraries represent an enormous investment of money and time. Data on the forty largest academic libraries in the United States in 1964–65 show operating expenditures in that year of $83

[1] Allan Cartter, *An Assessment of Quality in Graduate Education* (Washington: American Council on Education, 1966), p. 114.

million of which $48 million was spent for salaries and wages and
$29.5 million for books and other library materials. New volumes
added to collections numbered 3.6 million, at an approximate average cost of $8.25 per book. Staff in full-time equivalents numbered
8,023, with salaries averaging $6,000 per head. As might be expected,
about three-quarters of these outlays support acquisitions for the social sciences and humanities, reflecting their central position in the
development, control, and use of collections. How much of this
goes to history as opposed to other disciplines it is impossible to say,
if only because most books are of potential interest to more than
one discipline. It seems clear, however, that at any given point of
time, historians are the most active users of the collection.

GROWTH OF LIBRARIES

Many indices and statements attest to the almost exponential growth of users, their interests, and research materials over
nearly any time span of the twentieth century, and more particularly
in recent years. Such growth imposes increasing strains on traditional
library systems and makes new approaches and resources imperative.

The two major sources of pressure are the growing demand for
library materials and the even more rapidly increasing creation of
such materials.

Taking demand first, the most spectacular increase is the one from
four PhDs awarded in 1869 to 20,000 per year a century later.
Over the same period, college and university faculty members have
risen from 6,000 to nearly half a million; student population, from
52,000 to five million. This surge of numbers, however, tells only
part of the story. Equally important, especially in recent years, has
been the opening of new areas to investigation and instruction, most
prominently, the recognition of the importance to American scholars
and students of an awareness and knowledge of so-called exotic
areas: Soviet Russia and the socialist world in the period immediately
after the Second World War; the Third World of Latin America,
Africa, and Asia in the last decade. These new areas of coverage have
imposed a tremendous burden on library budgets. First, there has
been the costly process of catching up—acquiring the materials that
should have been purchased earlier. Then, there has been the cost
of a rapidly expanding flow of new material. All of this has been the
more difficult because of the special language skills required: it is

not easy to find cataloguers who know Chinese or Hindi; they can usually earn more doing other things.

At the same time, the changing techniques of research and areas of inquiry have created a demand for new kinds of research material: the whole range of photographic and electronic products, ranging from microfilms of material that would otherwise be unavailable, to the new world of machine-readable data in the form of tapes or cards. All of this has posed in turn new requirements for equipment to process, duplicate, or otherwise make use of this material.

This growth in demand is reinforced and aggravated by the pressure from the supply side. The use of new materials, for example, has as its counterpart the growing flow of such materials in response to, but also in anticipation of, rising demand. Thus, whereas originally most microfilm work was done on order to meet the specific needs of individual scholars, more and more publication is taking place in the form of microfilm, microfiches, or microcards as a way of making available to libraries and scholars material long since out of print and generally unavailable on the second-hand market. Newspapers, for example, are being filmed in this way on speculation—that is, in anticipation of orders—in a number of countries. Another instance is the Evans collection of all items published in the American colonies or the United States before 1815. These collections are invaluable. They are also extremely expensive, costing thousands of dollars for a single run, and eating up a substantial part of the budget of even the wealthiest libraries. Their availability, moreover, creates a demand by making it possible for scholars to add new dimensions to their investigations or undertake inquiries that would otherwise be impossible. They also provide material for instructional purposes and enhance the quality of graduate work while raising the expectations of student performance. From a costly luxury, custom-made for a specific purpose, these new photographic materials become a staple of the serious library collection. Magnetic tapes have not yet reached that stage, but if previous experience is any indication, they too will graduate from the private to the general.

Yet the photographic and electronic materials are only the glamorous frontier of library expansion. Output of conventional published materials follows the same upward curve. Apart from official publications, for instance, the number of book titles published in the United States alone rose from 13,462 in 1958 to 28,451 in 1964; that is, it more than doubled in six years. Foreign language materials, more and more important in United States research libraries, have been multiplying even faster. To take a single case, in 1950 the USSR published 52 titles on Latin America, but by 1963 the number of publications had risen to 888, a small but important part of the 17,863 Russian titles noted for 1963–64.[3] To compound the problem, all of these materials are getting more and more expensive, for book costs have outstripped the general course of inflation in every country. Ten years ago retail prices for scholarly books in the United States were running about a penny a page—give or take some for the cost of material, the presence of illustrations, and the style of printing. Today, three cents a page is usual and four or five cents not unusual, with reprints of older classics running even higher. Some of the latter, which are of particular importance to those newer libraries that are trying to fill gaps in their collections, are priced at ten cents and upwards per page, substantially more than the cost of photocopy reproduction.

Meanwhile there is the ever-vexatious problem of ephemera—most of these generated not by the traditional commercial or official sources of newspapers and books, but by the private sector. Organizations seeking to influence public affairs have proliferated, as each seeks to capture a larger share of potential public support. These have issued a wide variety of materials, some in standard periodical form, but more in the form of more ephemeral items—flyers, leaflets, brochures, and newsletters; these, in turn, constitute a new and vital part of the historical record. Yet, being ephemeral, the agencies which produce them rarely are preoccupied with their preservation for historical research, and, in turn, libraries have not taken them seriously enough as permanent records—they seem to have less importance than the public document or the scholarly journal—and have failed to develop acquisition programs necessary to gather and preserve them. Historians concerned with the systematic study of social change visualize such materials as providing insight into a far wider range of movements and values than can traditional materials. In turn, these demands require innovations in library programs.

This inflation of supply and demand, combined with the substantial increase in cost of acquisitions, to say nothing of rising salaries for personnel, has imposed on the nation's libraries a labor

    [3] Louis R. Wilson, "Introduction," in Jerrold Orne, ed., "Current Trends in Collection Development in University Libraries," Library Trends, XV, no. 2 (October, 1966), 197; Robert G. Carlton, ed., Latin America in Soviet Writings: A Bibliography [Hispanic Foundation Publications, nos. 1 and 2] (Baltimore: The Johns Hopkins Press, 1966), p. xii.

of Sisyphus. They buy and buy, yet never catch up. Some 2,140 college and university libraries reported that their aggregate holdings rose from 176.7 million volumes in 1959–60 to 227.1 million by 1963–64. Over the same period, the number of volumes added per year rose from 8.1 million to 13.6 million.[4] A series of studies based on independent data from 58 major research libraries analyzed many of these trends in detail. Taking fiscal year 1950 as a base, past experience to 1964 was extrapolated to 1980. The average period for doubling the number of volumes held is now seventeen years; it was further predicted that present rates of acquisition would double in nine to twelve years, and that costs would double every seven years.[5]

The projected impact on space and personnel needs seems almost self-evident. Even though growth rates of the collections at the larger and older libraries generally slacken from the 4–5 percent general rate to perhaps 2–3 percent, the influx of materials in all is large and absolute space requirements proportional. Thus at Harvard, every additional 100,000 volumes (about half the annual acquisition) requires 10,000 square feet of new floor space. At the same time, the needs of new users must be met: increased numbers of undergraduates, graduate students, faculty, and visiting scholars, all of whose requirements for use of collections differ.[6] The standard guide to planning academic and research library buildings suggests a minimum allotment of 25 square feet per undergraduate, 30 for first-year graduate students, 35–40 for those writing dissertations, with a preliminary estimate of 75 square feet of individual study space for faculty users, separate from their office space. The question arises, however, whether these guidelines are still valid. They rest on the assumption that present patterns of study and research are adequate and durable. Yet as we have argued above, the effective organization of scholarly inquiry and advanced instruction requires the development of a large number of small, special-purpose libraries, with facilities for

[4] Theodore Samore, *Library Statistics of Colleges and Universities, 1963–64: Analytic Report* (Washington: Government Printing Office, 1968), Table A, p. 5.
[5] O. C. Dunn, W. F. Seibert, and Janice A. Scheuneman, *The Past and Likely Future of 58 Research Libraries, 1951–1980: A Statistical Study of Growth and Change* (Lafayette, Ind.: Purdue University, Libraries and Audio-Visual Center, 1965), Figures 1–3.
[6] Keyes D. Metcalfe, *Planning Academic and Research Library Buildings* (New York, 1965), pp. 3–4, 99–104.

offices and desks for both teachers and students in contiguous areas
—a workshop-seminar comparable to the laboratory of the natural
sciences.

Just as space is short, so is personnel. Direct ratios between added
volumes and increase of staff are less simple than one would like,
given the wide variety of accounting and reporting practices. The
Purdue study cited above shows a predicted doubling of professional
staff at 15 to 17 year intervals between 1950 and 1980.[7] Whether
this will be sufficient is not at all clear. Specialized personnel do not
meet current needs, let alone those of burgeoning new and branch
academic libraries presently springing up at the rate of 100 a year
and estimated at 1,000 by the fall of 1975.[8]

In the face of these pressures, librarians have been forced to ever
more desperate remedies. At Harvard University, where the library is
a national resource and attracts every year thousands of scholars
from this country and abroad, the lack of funds has more or less
imposed an abandonment of what is called retrospective buying,
that is, the acquisition of earlier material in order to fill gaps in the
collection. At the same time, the effort to keep up with needs in
exotic areas has led to a constriction of expenditures on materials
dealing with more familiar parts of the world. At the University of
California, Berkeley, the inability of the catalogue department to
keep up with the flow of new acquisitions has long imposed serious
limitations on the flow of information to users, while the shortage
of space has led to the practice of shelving books by size rather
than by subject, thereby vitiating the stack privilege that is one of
the great advantages of the American researcher by comparison with
his foreign counterpart. Everywhere, space in library buildings is at
a premium, with the result that even in those institutions where
desks were once available to scholars among the shelves, this privilege
is either being eroded or has become available to a diminishing
portion of users. At the same time, the lack of space for new
acquisitions has led an increasing number of libraries to disperse their
collections at considerable sacrifice of their usefulness. Here, to be
sure, the new technology of microfilm and microprint has made possible some economies of storage; but it has also created new space
requirements to accommodate the reading and reproduction equipment.

[7] Dunn, Seibert, and Scheuneman, *The Past and Likely Future*, Figure 5.
[8] Samore, *Library Statistics*, p. 4.

LIBRARY NEEDS AND OPPORTUNITIES

In the light of the discussion above, the following requirements and opportunities seem to us of paramount importance:

Personnel

The changing nature of the library, the increased variety of its holdings, and the diversification of its services call for new specialists. Most major libraries have made major advances in automated services and have hired personnel competent in this area. Similar progress has not been made, however, in training curatorial librarians who combine knowledge of subject and area with skill in library techniques and can thus work with scholars in planning and executing programs responsive to new intellectual interests. Specialized acquisitions personnel remain one of the weakest links in the library system. Especially needed are persons who are themselves scholars and thus aware of innovations in scholarship, so that they can compensate by their knowledge and interests for the inevitable gaps in faculty initiative. All the great libraries have had people of this kind, but they are becoming scarcer—partly because the best of them are diverted into administrative or teaching jobs, partly because the salaries for this kind of work are not commensurate with the talent and contributions of these specialists. There is clearly a need here to define and institutionalize a new career with sufficient rewards in money and prestige to attract the talent required.

Criteria of Selection and Specialization of Collections

Given the limitations of funds and personnel, the question of choice of acquisitions becomes a crucial one for every library: even the richest and greatest admit that they cannot hope to acquire a comprehensive collection of all types of library materials. The dilemma is to balance collections to meet basic needs of teaching and research at any given institution with cooperative participation in regional or national facilities where many institutions share the cost. It must be emphasized that such joint facilities must not become an excuse for the underdevelopment of local resources: easy availability remains a primary stimulus of library use. Yet they can effectively supplement these resources and they do provide desperately needed space for overflow.

Other efforts to economize have taken the form of the allocation of responsibility for specified kinds of materials to different libraries. The aim has been to insure that some one institution pick up as many as possible of the publications in a given area, rather than leave this to the hazard of local acquisition policy and budgets. One of the earliest of these programs was the Farmington Plan (1944–), which assigned responsibility for acquisitions by country of publication. This has been followed by the Public Law 480 Program (1961–), the Higher Education Act of 1965, the Title IIC Program of shared cataloguing, and the incipient Material Development Program of the Association of Research Libraries, which is to provide greater availability of highly specialized research materials. Looking toward a larger, national design, the president appointed in 1967 a National Advisory Commission on Libraries, whose recommendations have not yet appeared.

In general the voices of scholarship have not been heard clearly in the formulation of these plans. Most professional associations have been content with asking for more, without specifying what or offering compelling justifications. So far as is known, no professional group in the social sciences or humanities has drawn up a rigorous set of requirements and guidelines to help the library community help them. Such aid as has been given has tended to be sporadic, unsystematic, individualistic, and generally ineffective.

Financial Support

More serious has been the failure to support such programs of cooperation or specialization with adequate financial resources. It is simply not enough to make the money currently available go further by rationalizing its allocation. What is needed is a commitment to the maintenance of the quality of the major national collections, and this implies, even in a context of distributed responsibilities, a substantial increase in funding. The great libraries of the United States constitute an incomparable national resource. Unlike their analogues abroad, their collections are international in scope rather than parochial, and their usefulness for comparative research is enhanced by their easy accessibility. Nowhere else in the world are open stacks and borrowing privileges so readily available;

just as nowhere else are catalogue arrangements, reference services, and similar facilities—for all their faults—so convenient and efficient. Insofar as the present report, therefore, criticizes the weaknesses of the American university library system, it does so by comparison with what could and should be, not with what is to be found in other parts of the world. It is a commonplace of scholarship that researchers working on problems that require travel abroad should complete all possible reading in this country before leaving for the field, on the ground that one can work here two or three times as fast as in any foreign center. Our great libraries constitute, therefore, not only a great intellectual treasure, but a form of labor-saving capital.

This stock of capital must not be allowed to run down. Since it is now abundantly clear that even with the best of will, the universities are no longer able to maintain their libraries at traditional levels of completeness and efficiency, outside assistance must be made available. What is needed is a commitment of the federal government to the support and development of great regional library centers, as well as to the promotion of a larger number of specialized units throughout the country. These great centers would continue to be an integral part of the universities to which they are attached, but their regional and even national role would be recognized— the logical counterpart of outside support—and provision would be made for the regular accommodation of visiting scholars. In some areas, it might be necessary to build such a center *de novo*; but where existing libraries are rich enough to provide a substantial basis for such a collection, it would be advisable to develop one or more of these for the purpose. Essentially, these libraries would be comparable to, though certainly less costly than, the great regional installations that have been built for research in particle physics in various parts of the country.

Storage, Retrieval and Use

Efficient though the present system of retrieval may be by comparison with the older techniques found in other countries (the great foreign libraries rely on bound repertories with paste-in entries or incomplete published lists and sometimes not even that), it obviously falls far short of what modern technology has already made possible. There is no reason any longer why scholars should have to spend considerable time preparing bibliographies, checking card entries, hunting up missing items in the published lists of other collections, and obtaining some books only through the tedious process of circular inquiry through interlibrary borrowing. Thanks to computer technology, it is now theoretically possible to produce a machine-readable union catalogue that would satisfy the following criteria:

a. It would include all works available anywhere in the United States and give location.

b. It would include articles and other parts of larger wholes.

c. It could index items by subject, time period, and geographical area.

d. It would produce printouts of bibliographical lists on request.

e. It would provide responses to distant users through console connections.

f. It would tie in with microprint arrangements, so that users could obtain copies of specified pages as well as bibliographical information.

This is the theoretical ideal. Some of this is still a long way off—the last item especially. Even so, exploration of these opportunities is already being undertaken, particularly by the Library of Congress in its project MARC (Machine Readable Cataloguing), its RECON (Retrospective Conversion) Pilot Project and its allied automation programs (LOCATE, IRIS, START).[9] As yet, limitations of budget, urgency, and available machine capability have confined the MARC program to English-language publications in specified subject areas and a small number of cooperating libraries. These early experiments have shown that the use of computer tapes is not an "open sesame" to a bibliographical paradise. It entails a commitment to a certain mode of organizing the information, so that while "some aspects of the machine record can be changed to suit individual problems, others are quite inflexible."[10] All of this points up once again the fact that the research community must define more rigorously their present and anticipated needs so that they can be accommodated in a national systems design.

[9] See Paul R. Reimers, "Progress in Automation," in Dagmar H. Perman, ed., *Bibliography and the Historian* (Santa Barbara, Calif.: Clio Press, 1968), pp. 57–67; also the *Annual Report of the Librarian of Congress for the Fiscal Year Ending June 30, 1968* (Washington, 1969), pp. 5–7.

[10] Reimers, "Progress in Automation," p. 80.

THE SPECIAL PROBLEM OF ARCHIVES
AND MUSEUMS

Everything we have said so far about libraries and books applies, with appropriate changes, to archives and museums and their collections. These repositories face the same exponential growth in the volume of objects worthy of preservation and in the costs of custodianship. It is not only that modern communications technology generates an ever larger stream of paper (despite the telephone), but that our conception of what constitutes appropriate matter for preservation is broadening all the time. This is particularly true for social science, which is learning to utilize material that was once considered trivial or banal for the illumination of problems that were once considered trivial or banal. Once the scholar takes all human behavior as his province, once he moves out of the exalted spheres of power into the everyday lives of ordinary people, once he interests himself in the banalities of culture as well as the peak performances and in the thought of the many as well as the genius of the few, he must scrutinize and understand a whole range of artifacts and documents that were once thought of as expendable.

The implications are obvious. Archival repositories and museums need substantially increased support to continue their conventional tasks and to assume new ones appropriate to the intellectual interests of the future. Museums in particular need funds to enable them to serve as more than storage warehouses and display cases. They have to serve students and scholars by establishing those conditions that will enable visitors to become users. This development will entail for some curators a drastic change in their conception of the material in their custody and of their custodial function. Too many today—more often abroad, it should be said, than in the United States—think of themselves as guardians, protecting the treasures of the past from the conscious and unconscious vandals of the present. There will always be vandals, and curators will always have to guard against them. But as the character of archival and museum collections changes and with it their clientele, these protective functions will have to yield to those of service and collaboration.

The preservation and scholarly utilization of motion picture films furnishes a good example of the kind of rethinking required. There is no need here to dwell on the significance of films as a historical source for tomorrow's scholars. The current generation has been formed in large part by motion pictures and television, and even if one is not prepared to adopt the views of a McLuhan, one must recognize that we have here the raw material for a history (indeed a psychohistory) of popular culture, as well as a visual record of the events and mores of our time.

This implies the necessity of preserving the film in such a way as to make it available to students and scholars. It also suggests that the history of the future may not confine itself to the conventional verbal forms, that the film may turn out to be a medium of historical expression. To this end, film archives should be organized not only to serve the needs of courses of instruction in visual arts and communications and to furnish matter for entertainment, but also as a bank on which students, teachers, and scholars can draw for source material and cinematographic assistance. The time may come when part of a history dissertation takes the form of a documentary film prepared by the student. (It goes without saying that for that day to come, the viewing fees presently charged by most archives would have to be drastically reduced.)

The historical potential of a new medium of expression like film raises the larger question of the criteria that ought to guide the selection of material to be preserved for future generations of scholars. In view of the proliferation mentioned above, some selection is necessary; otherwise man will smother under the weight of his own records. At present there is little standardization of procedure even in regard to the obvious items: the papers of government, for example, or of business enterprises. In spite of efforts by archives and records commissions, public and private, much is still left to personal whim (most officials continue to take with them when they leave office the bulk of their important papers) and chance. Even when a preservation program has been agreed upon, legal requirements, physical constraints, and cultural lag continue to shape and distort decisions on what to keep and what to destroy.

Here, obviously, the historian of today can be of immense service to the historian of tomorrow. Instead of offering advice on criteria of selection when asked to do so, scholars should be taking the initiative and developing a rational program of preservation, which should be altered periodically as changing interests and circumstances require. To be sure, such a program will never be able to anticipate all the needs of the future; but it should prove more effective in this regard than the anarchy that now prevails. Even those

papers whose very bulk seems to destine them for destruction—
school records (including notes of guidance counselors and minutes
of conferences with parents), for example—could be selectively preserved on a systematic, regular basis. It is the everyday, routine
paperwork and artifacts that are the most voluminous, most familiar,
most cumbersome, and most easily spared. Yet if the historian of
the future is to understand what life was like for the great mass of
the population, the historian, the archivist and the curator of today
must find ways to preserve a rationally determined sample of this
material.

RECOMMENDATIONS

1. The United States government should commit itself,
as a matter of policy, to the maintenance and promotion of the
nation's research libraries as a national resource; this commitment
should entail the maintenance and enhancement of the coverage and
accessibility of the great reference collections.

2. The federal government, in cooperation with representatives
of the professional associations and research libraries, should plan
and fund a program for the development of major regional library
centers of roughly comparable quality, allowing for variations and
specializations in the content of collections. For reasons of economy
of money and personnel these centers should build when possible on
existing collections. They should include facilities for the reception
of visiting scholars, whom they should be able to bring and serve
without neglecting their obligations to resident teachers and students.
The cost of such support initially (not of construction costs) would
be of the order of $10 million (for seven or eight centers). In subse-
quent years, the start-up outlays would diminish, but operating costs
for acquisitions and services would grow in compensation.

3. *Libraries as Research Facilities.* Agencies financing historical
research should take some responsibility for the support of libraries,
both through direct grants to libraries for facilities and acquisitions,
particularly of hard-to-handle ephemera, and through grants to researchers for the acquisition of special collections of books, films,
documents, photographs, tapes, newspapers, and other materials es-
sential to their work, on condition that those materials be deposited
in libraries.

4. *Pooling of Materials.* The same agencies should encourage or

require recipients of grants to collect and deposit their historical materials in a form accessible to other investigators. This could be accomplished, among other ways, by (a) standardizing the forms in which data are recorded and classified; (b) offering attractive supplementary grants (for example, covering the costs of detailed inventories of materials) to historians willing to deposit their films, files, newspapers, and so on; or (c) awarding grants for the specific purpose of collecting certain kinds of materials from historians who have accumulated them.

5. The federal government, in cooperation with representatives of the libraries and professional associations, should create a machine-readable union catalogue, initially of all holdings in the United States, eventually of holdings abroad as well. The catalogue should lend itself to retrieval by subject as well as by author and title. It is impossible to establish at this time the cost of such a project, which might take two or more decades to convert existing records and catch up with current output. Inflation would certainly increase today's costs; gains in computer productivity and other technological advances might compensate for the increase. John Rather of the Library of Congress estimates a minimum of $24 million to edit and convert the National Union Catalogue and produce a machine-readable author catalogue of 12 million entries. The kind of catalogue we recommend would be two or three times that large and that much costlier. There would also be substantial outlays for the computer hardware and software required. Once the system was in operation, maintenance costs might be recovered in whole or part from users' fees.[11]

6. One or more schools of library training should create, in conjunction with the other faculties of their institutions, combined degree programs for curatorial personnel, who would receive training in a substantive discipline as well as in librarianship. (Such programs would be analogous to existing degree programs combining education and a selected discipline, like the Harvard Master of Arts in

---

[11] These calculations are based on the report of the RECON Working Task Force, *Conversion of Retrospective Catalog Records to Machine-Readable Form: A Study of the Feasibility of a National Bibliographic Service* (Washington: Library of Congress, 1969); and on a letter from John C. Rather of February 11, 1970. Rather suggests that in view of the uncertainties of these cost calculations, no estimates be offered at this time. But it is hard to see how any serious commitment to this task can be undertaken without some preliminary projections, however approximate.

Teaching.) Or research libraries might offer such a program in conjunction with the teaching departments of nearby universities.

7. The American Historical Association, in collaboration with the National Archives and the Smithsonian Institute, should collaborate in the formulation of criteria of selection of records and artifacts for preservation; and the federal government and private funding agencies should provide increased resources to accommodate the material so selected and to convert it where necessary into such forms (microfilm, microfiche, tape recordings) as will facilitate access and use by students and scholars. As a preliminary to the formulation of these criteria, historians should undertake two projects: (a) sample surveys of the gaps in the records and objects that have come down to us from selected earlier periods (what do we wish had been saved?); (b) a study and evaluation of the choices earlier generations have made of objects and records worthy of preservation in "time capsules" and similar samples (how good are the people of one period at foreseeing what their descendants will want to know about them?).

8
CONCLUSION AND FINAL RECOMMENDATIONS

This report has been aimed at two audiences: the historical profession; and those outside the profession, in government, in the academy, and in agencies promoting scholarship whose cooperation is necessary to achieve the goals set out above. This in itself makes the report of the History Panel different from those of the other panels of the Behavioral and Social Sciences Survey. The other panels did not have to persuade their colleagues of the worth of social and behavioral science or to define their identity as social scientists. There was a time when some of these disciplines agonized about such questions and fought internecine wars over such issues as the legitimacy of mathematical models or behaviorist research. But most of the dust has now settled, and the other social sciences have long since learned to live with equations and numbers and regression analysis and the unconscious.

Historians—or at least many historians—have not yet learned to live with these uncomfortable intruders on a world of art, intuition, and verbal skill; hence our concern at numerous points to stress the fact that we are speaking here for just one branch of the historical profession and our conviction that the changes we recommend are complementary to, rather than competitive with, other branches of historical scholarship. Social-scientific research will make history richer, more exciting, more valuable, more relevant (that much overused word!) to contemporary concerns and problems. But it is not alone in possessing these merits and much of what it has to contribute is dependent on its incorporation within the discipline of history. The flow of knowledge and insight here runs two ways. History has always been a borrower from other disciplines, and in

142

that sense social-scientific history is just another example of a time-honored process; but history has also been a lender, and all the social sciences would be immeasurably poorer without knowledge of the historical record. The social sciences are not a self-contained system, one of whose boundaries lies in some fringe area of the historical sciences. Rather the study of man is a continuum, and social-scientific history is a bridge between the social sciences and the humanities.

What we are proposing, to both audiences, is a bigger and better bridge.

The following recommendations sum up those offered in the earlier chapters:

1. Departments of history should diversify and enrich the present program of instruction: by building more courses around analytical themes (war, population, urbanization, and the like); by providing training in the techniques and concepts of social science (including quantitative methods and computer analysis); and by adding to the instructional staff, on a part-time and full-time basis, specialists in these techniques and concepts. Training in these areas should be required of those students intending to specialize in social-scientific history; but all history concentrators and graduate students should be required to do a substantial portion of their work in some other discipline or disciplines.

2. Universities and colleges, with the support of public and private funding agencies, should increase the support available for graduate study in history to a level commensurate with that found in the other social sciences. In particular, support is needed for the extra time required for training in related disciplines and quantitative techniques; for the application of these methods in research (equipment, computer time, photographic work); and for a more flexible arrangement of field research.

3. Departments of history should organize a substantial part of graduate education, for those students who desire it, around the continuing workshop-seminar. Such a seminar would be an analogue to the teaching laboratory of the natural sciences: it would have its own premises, its own specialized library and store of research material, its own research equipment, and it would unite faculty, staff, and students in a changing variety of individual and team research projects built around a common interest, more or less broadly defined. The members of such a seminar could also serve as the staff

for undergraduate courses in its area of interest, thereby gaining experience in teaching as well as research.

4. Universities and colleges, with the support of public and private funding agencies, should make it easier for historians to continue learning and research after the doctorate. Specifically, we recommend a loosening of leave arrangements to allow for both shorter and longer leaves than those currently permitted; the establishment of the postdoctoral research appointment as a normal option for first step on the academic ladder (as it already is in other disciplines); a program of retraining grants in combination with the establishment of interuniversity training institutes in fields important to historical research (statistics, computer programming, psychoanalysis); and increased support for such research centers as the Center for Advanced Study in the Behavioral Sciences and the creation of new ones, both in this country and abroad.

5. Universities and colleges, with the assistance of public and private funding agencies, should promote those forms of cooperation that will enrich their programs of instruction and facilitate research: specifically, interuniversity research consortia, conferences, discussion groups, collaborative teaching, joint degrees, and division of labor in the acquisition of equipment and materials. All these forms of cooperation are already established in various places on both an ad hoc and a standing basis; but there is still a great deal that can be done, particularly on an international level.

6. Public and private funding agencies should promote cooperation between American and foreign historical scholarship by linking counterpart grants for foreign scholars to American travel stipends; and American scholars working abroad should similarly promote cooperation where possible and appropriate by affiliating themselves with foreign academic institutions, by involving native scholars in their research, and by communicating their techniques and findings to the scholars and students of the host country.

7. The federal government should commit itself to the maintenance and growth of our major libraries and archives as a precious national resource; and it should develop additional regional libraries so that colleges and universities throughout the country will be within convenient reach of a major repository. Further, the federal government should finance the preparation of a machine-readable union catalogue of all library holdings in the United States, including eventually articles in periodicals and collective works, with entries retrievable by subject as well as by author and title.

8. Libraries, archives, and museums should widen the range of their collections to include those everyday records and artifacts that are now disposed of and destroyed but that will one day be the staple source material of social-scientific history; historians should join with librarians and curators in developing a program for the systematic collection, storage, and retrieval of such material; and public and private funding agencies should finance both the planning and implementation of this expanded curatorial function.

APPENDIX A

HISTORY DEPARTMENTS PARTICIPATING IN THE DEPARTMENTAL QUESTIONNAIRE SURVEY

University of Alabama
American University
University of Arizona
Arizona State University
Ball State University
Boston College
Boston University
Brandeis University
Brigham Young University
Brown University
Bryn Mawr College
University of California, Berkeley
University of California, Davis
University of California, Los Angeles*
University of California, Riverside
University of California, Santa Barbara
Case Western Reserve University *
Catholic University of America*
University of Chicago
University of Cincinnati
City University of New York
Claremont Graduate School
Clark University
University of Colorado*
Columbia University
University of Connecticut
Cornell University*
University of Delaware
University of Denver

Duke University
Emory University
University of Florida
Florida State University
Fordham University
George Peabody College for Teachers
George Washington University
Georgetown University
University of Georgia
Harvard University
University of Hawaii
University of Houston
Howard University
University of Idaho
University of Illinois
University of Indiana
University of Iowa
Johns Hopkins University
University of Kansas*
Kansas State University
University of Kentucky
Lehigh University
Louisiana State University
Loyola University
University of Maine
University of Maryland
University of Massachusetts
University of Michigan
Michigan State University

* An asterisk indicates non-response to the questionnaire.

146

University of Minnesota
Mississippi State University
University of Missouri at Columbia
University of Nebraska
University of New Mexico*
New York University
State University of New York at Albany
State University of New York at Buffalo
University of North Carolina
Northwestern University
University of Notre Dame
Ohio University*
Ohio State University
University of Oklahoma
University of Oregon
University of the Pacific*
University of Pennsylvania
Pennsylvania State University
University of Pittsburgh
Princeton University
Rice University
University of Rochester
Rutgers, The State University

St. John's University
St. Louis University*
University of South Carolina
University of Southern California
University of Southern Mississippi
Stanford University
Syracuse University
Temple University
University of Tennessee
University of Texas, Austin
Texas Christian University
Texas Technological College
Tufts University
Tulane University
University of Utah*
Vanderbilt University
University of Virginia
University of Washington
Washington State University
Washington University
Wayne State University
West Virginia University
University of Wisconsin, Madison
University of Wyoming
Yale University

APPENDIX B

TECHNICAL NOTE ON THE SPECIAL SURVEY OF HISTORIANS

During the winter of 1967–68, the members of the History Panel decided to submit a special questionnaire to members of the largest American university departments of history and of a few departments selected for other reasons. The questionnaire was to deal especially with the involvement of working historians in behavioral and social science fields. It was to include a number of items which would lend themselves to quantitative description and comparison, as well as a smaller number of items calling for free discussion. The questionnaire went through a number of drafts in February and March. We mailed a preliminary version to members of the history department of Indiana University in April, 1968. On the basis of the early returns from that mailing, we made some minor revisions in the questionnaire.

The main mailing went to members of twenty-eight other departments in May, and the bulk of the returns came in during June and early July. Several weeks after the initial mailing, we sent reminders to all those who had not replied, enclosing a postcard for early response.

The twenty-nine history departments polled included (a) the twenty departments rated highest in the Cartter report on the quality of graduate education in the United States, (b) the three departments not on the first list which were among the twenty largest producers of PhDs in history during the years 1960 to 1966, and (c) six other departments selected to represent good schools of several other varieties: Notre Dame, Howard, Carleton, Reed, Smith, and Swarthmore. Our membership lists for these departments contained a total of 1,001 names—about 35 per department.[1] Although we have calculated the response rates presented

---

[1] Most of the lists omitted instructors, who are often graduate students teaching part time and who normally hold short-term appointments. Our sample therefore drastically underrepresents a significant (and probably discontented) segment of the profession.

below over the full 1,001 historians, at least 52 persons on the list *could not* have answered because they had died, retired or left the university. Altogether, 597 historians sent back usable questionnaires; just under 60 percent of the full list, about 63 percent of those actually eligible to reply. Another 32 persons sent letters, some of them responding to the general themes of the questionnaire, and others explaining their refusal to fill it out. If we were to count these as replies, the total would be 629, some 63 percent of the full list. For a mailed questionnaire with one reminder, the 60 percent return is good, but not overwhelming. It is low enough to offer some risk of selective response to the questionnaire.

Altogether, the historians to whom we sent the questionnaire gave four kinds of responses, singly or in combination: they filled it out and returned it, they sent back our reminder card with some explanation of their not having replied, they sent a letter, or they did not reply at all. The major breakdown is this:

Sent in usable questionnaire	597
Sent card only	115
Sent letter, but no questionnaire	32
No response whatsoever	259
Total	1,001

Of the 147 persons from whom (or on whose behalf) we received a card and/or a letter but no questionnaire, 52 were unavailable through death or absence, 40 refused to answer the questionnaire (some of them with considerable élan), and 55 indicated their intention to answer when they had a chance. We have counted as "refusals" the ten persons who (or whose secretaries) returned blank questionnaires without explanation, plus those who gave the following replies:

Too busy, not enough time	15
Too tired	2
Never answer questionnaires	3
Questionnaires are useless	1
This questionnaire is too long	1
These questions are impossible to answer	2
Uninterested	1
Consider it an invasion of privacy	2
Resent depersonalization of questionnaire	2
Allergic to questionnaires	1
Total	30

In short, a handful of the thousand historians polled vigorously rejected the survey, 50 or 60 promised to fill in the questionnaire but never got around to it, another several hundred did not bother to reply, but the great majority took the whole thing seriously and with good grace.[2] For the individual departments, the returns went as follows:

Institution	Number of Questonnaires Sent	Number Returned	Percent Returned
University of California, Berkeley	63	32	50.8%
University of California, Los Angeles	54	31	57.4
Carleton College	8	3	37.5
University of Chicago	71	39	54.9
Columbia University	69	30	43.5
Cornell University	21	17	81.0
Duke University	24	16	66.7
Georgetown University	19	10	52.6
Harvard University	48	37	77.1
Johns Hopkins University	11	9	81.8
Howard University	12	4	33.3
University of Illinois	26	17	65.4
Indiana University	53	37	69.8
University of Michigan	46	22	47.8
University of Minnesota	28	21	75.0
New York University	41	22	53.7
University of N. Carolina, Chapel Hill	34	24	70.6
Northwestern University	22	12	54.5
University of Notre Dame	25	14	56.0
University of Pennsylvania	18	8	44.4
Princeton University	47	33	70.2
Reed College	12	9	75.0
Smith College	22	10	45.5
Stanford University	35	19	54.3
Swarthmore College	11	11	100.0
University of Texas	21	10	47.6
University of Washington	36	23	63.9
University of Wisconsin	58	35	60.3
Yale University	66	42	63.6
Total	1,001	597	59.6

Nothing obvious distinguishes the high-response departments (Cornell, Harvard, Hopkins, Minnesota, Chapel Hill, Princeton, Reed, Swath-

[2] In addition to the care with which our respondents filled out the short-answer section of the questionnaire, one sign of their interest is the fact that over nine-tenths of them provided a long-hand answer to at least one of the inquiries in the final, discursive section.

more) from the low-response ones (Carleton, Columbia, Howard, Michigan, Penn, Smith, Texas).

In order to identify the response bias by field, we arbitrarily selected six departments from the list for which we had current catalogs matching members of the department with the courses they taught. We attempted to classify those who were on our mailing list and in the catalog in terms of geographic area, period, and subject of specialization, using courses taught as evidence.[3] We can tabulate the response by geographic area and institution in this way:

PERCENT RETURNING USABLE QUESTIONNAIRES BY AREA

Institution	Europe	North America	Latin America	Asia/Africa
Berkeley (N = 52)	50	38	67	36
Cornell (N = 21)	80	75	0	50
Illinois (N = 25)	50	40	100	75
Notre Dame (N = 16)	67	67	100	—
Smith (N = 21)	64	0	100	0
Washington (N = 34)	47	67	100	100
Total (N = 169)	60	48	78	63

Of course, some of these figures are based on one or two persons, and do not deserve attention. The overall tendency, however, is fairly clear. People in the less traditional fields were more likely to reply to the questionnaire. Historians of North America showed the least interest. Since people in the newer fields are also somewhat more open to social scientific history than their fellows, this means that our sample over-represents historians with an active interest in BASS. Few people will find this surprising, but it warns us to extend our descriptive findings to all historians in the departments polled only with caution. (Even less should we take the findings as a description of all historians in the U.S., since we have deliberately emphasized the most prestigious and active graduate departments.)

Here are the response rates by time period:

American:
Colonial and Revolutionary   43%
Early National   65
Civil War–World War I   47
World War I–present   63

[3] This is far from foolproof, since some standard courses (historiography, for example) do not lend themselves to this sort of classification, and some instructors (especially junior men and members of the smaller departments) do not teach subjects they regard as their specialties. For those historians classified this way from whom we also had a questionnaire classifying themselves, we found an agreement of 88 percent on geographic area, 64 percent on period, and only 42 percent on specialization.

Non-American:

Ancient	70
Medieval	50
Early Modern	54
Modern (1789–1914)	49
Twentieth Century	71

And here are the response rates by our least reliable classification, special field:

General survey	57%
Diplomatic, international	71
Intellectual, art	36
Political, constitutional	55
Social, economic	67
Science, technology	71
Other (church, ethnic, exploration, frontier, teaching of history, military)	33

Again it appears that historians in untraditional fields, and in fields already having strong connections with the behavioral and social sciences, were more inclined than their fellows to answer the questionnaire. All in all, we have to treat our sample as slightly biased in favor of BASS involvement and interest.

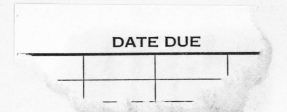